SUPER SKILLS FOR SUPER KIDS

DISCOVER YOUR STRENGTHS, MAKE FRIENDS, AND EXPERIENCE NEW ADVENTURES!

Maria Dawn

Special ArT

Super Skills for Super Kids
Discover Your Strengths, Make Friends, and Experience New Adventures!

© 2024 by Maria Dawn, Special Art
All rights reserved. No part of this publication may be reproduced, distributed, or transmitted in any form or by any means, including photocopying, recording, or other electronic or mechanical methods, without the prior written permission of the publisher, except for brief quotations in reviews or non-commercial uses permitted by copyright law. For permissions, contact: support@specialartbooks.com.

Published by Special Art Books
www.specialartbooks.com

Paperback ISBN: 9791255531593

Cover Illustration by Maria Francesca Perifano
Image Credits: Shutterstock

This book is intended for informational purposes only and is not a substitute for professional advice. Readers should consult a qualified professional regarding medical, financial, or other decisions. Neither the author nor the publisher shall be liable for any damages or actions taken based on the information provided in this book.

Table of Contents

Foreword vii

Introduction 1

Part 1: Personal Skills

Chapter One: You Have Superpowers! 4

Why You Should Know Your Super Skills 6
Turning Weaknesses into Strengths and Learning New Skills 7
What You've Learned in This Chapter 9
List of Superpowers 10

Chapter Two: Why Do You Feel and Act This Way? 12

A Positive Attitude Equals a Positive Experience 12
The Pause Button: Thinking Before You Act 15
Your Super Alter Ego: Becoming Your Inner Hero 18
When It's Time to Get Support or Change Your Life 20
What You've Learned in This Chapter 22

Chapter Three: Navigating Change and Loss 24

What Is Grief and How Do You Overcome It? 26
What's on the "Other Side"? 28
Living and Loving 29
Things You Can Do to Get Through Grief 30
What You've Learned in This Chapter 32

Chapter Four: Making Super Decisions 33

The Super Skill of Making Good Decisions 35
What You've Learned in This Chapter 39

Chapter Five: Setting Goals to Achieve Your Dreams   40

    The Difference Between Goals and Dreams   41
    Dream Big: Getting Going with Goals   45
    Setting Some Goals Right Now   46
    What You've Learned in This Chapter   47

Part 2: Social Skills

Chapter Six: Becoming a Communication Superhero   50

    The Power of Body Language: Non-verbal Cues   51
    Dressing the Part   53
    What You Say and How You Say It Matters   53
    Ask and Receive: The Importance of Clear Communication   55
    The Silent Movie Exercise   56
    What You've Learned in This Chapter   57

Chapter Seven: Spreading Kindness   58

    Why Are People Mean?   59
    Remembering Who You Are—A Superstar   61
    Walking in Someone Else's Shoes   62
    What You've Learned in This Chapter   65

Part 3: Practical Skills

Chapter Eight: Dealing with Emergencies   68

    Emergency Basics: Be Prepared and Stay Calm   68
    Real-Life Scenarios: Falls, Fires, and More   70
    Wounds and Injuries   70
    Stroke   71
    Heart Attack   71
    Epileptic Attack   71
    The House Is On Fire   72
    How to Extinguish a Fire   73
    When to Leave the House   74

Table of Contents

    What You've Learned in This Chapter   **75**

Chapter Nine: Becoming a Chore Master   **77**

    Mastering Your Chores   **77**
    Check the Facts Before You Begin   **78**
    Safe and Sound: Using Appliances with Care   **79**
    The Cleaning Game: Making Cleaning and Tidying Up Fun!   **79**
    Laundry   **79**
    Washing Dishes   **80**
    Cleaning the Floors   **81**
    Dusting   **81**
    Other Chores   **81**
    What You've Learned in This Chapter   **82**

Chapter Ten: Becoming a Super Foodie   **83**

    The Foods That Make Your Body Happy   **83**
    Read the Label   **84**
    Kitchen Tools 101   **86**
    Learning to Make the Recipes You Love—Family Cooking Fun   **87**
    Easy Treats—Cooking Made Simple   **87**
    What You've Learned in This Chapter   **91**

Chapter Eleven: Saving, Spending, and Other Money Matters   **92**

    The Jar Method: Knowing Where Your Money Goes   **93**
    Budgeting: Knowing How to Spend Well   **95**
    What You've Learned in This Chapter   **96**

Chapter Twelve: Owning Your Time: Time Management and Study Skills   **97**

    Scheduling Like a Pro—Making Time Work for You   **98**
    Sharpen Your Mind: Focus and Concentration   **99**
    What You've Learned in This Chapter   **104**

Chapter Thirteen: Digital Superheroes: Navigating the Online World Safely   105

    Social Media Anxiety   106
    When to Post, When Not to Post   107
    Connecting with Cool People and Controlling Your Privacy   108
    Negative Comments and Posts   110
    AI—Artificial Intelligence   111
    What You've Learned in This Chapter   115

Chapter Fourteen: Becoming an Eco-Warrior: Protecting Our Planet Together   117

    Practical Steps for Environmental Superheroes   118
    What You've Learned in This Chapter   120

Conclusion   121

    Your Super Skills Journey Continues   121

Foreword

I am delighted to introduce *Super Skills for Super Kids: Discover Your Strengths, Make Friends, and Experience New Adventures!* In my three decades as a psychologist, child developmentalist, educator, and parent coach, my overarching goal has remained the same—to promote optimal outcomes for kids. I believe the most powerful way to do this is to bring research into practical application. Growing up is a universal, yet immense task. It is indeed an adventure and our children need all the help they can get to be prepared for this critically important journey. This book is exemplary in the service of that mission through offering young readers a comprehensive guide to essential life skills.

Maria Dawn accomplishes this by drawing on her varied and inspiring personal and professional background. She uses humor and deep insight to help children discover and sharpen the super skills within every child. Age-appropriate, evidence-based, and engaging, *Super Skills for Super Kids* is both accessible and enjoyable for children. Readers will feel encouraged and empowered through the supportive rather than admonishing tone. As they explore its pages, children will gain a wealth of knowledge and practical skills, including self-awareness, setting and achieving goals, building and maintaining good relationships, effective communication, time management, handling emergencies, understanding the importance of health and wellness, navigating the online world, and more.

The book is chock full of real-world examples and stories (often humorous!) that bring the content to life. Children are encouraged to apply what they learn in meaningful ways as each topic is skillfully balanced with practical exercises and activities. Children will recognize and develop their unique assets and skills through utilizing everyday moments and turning these into opportunities for self-discovery, competence, and confidence.

That each child has individual strengths, yet shares the need to build foundational skills essential for a happy and successful life, clearly comes through in the pages of this book. We all want our children to be well-equipped to face their challenges in the moment and those that lie ahead. I highly recommend *Super Skills for Super Kids* to children, and to parents and educators. It is an outstanding resource that not only promotes all aspects of development from emotional to social to academic, it also inspires self-confidence and a sense of adventure in young readers.

Sincerely,
Lilla Dale McManis, MEd, PhD
Psychologist and Educator

Introduction

You might hate school.

You might love school.

Either way, unless you attend a *very* special school, chances are they aren't teaching you how to believe in yourself outside of academics or deal with life in general.

In fact, you were probably pretty lucky if they taught you how to tie your shoelaces in school.

And, yet, we can all agree that knowing how to tie your shoelaces is essential for life.

So is building good relationships.

Knowing what to do in an emergency.

Knowing how to talk to adults to make them actually *listen*.

Knowing what foods make you happy and healthy and what foods don't.

Lots of things are *essential* for a happy life. And, unfortunately, school doesn't teach very many of them.

Alright, so that's not entirely true. Some schools today have started incorporating some of these things in their curriculums as they realize their importance. And some teachers are true super heroes—doing everything they can to help you become the best person you can be. It's just, most schools still don't have the resources to teach all of this.

That's why this book exists! To help you and, perhaps, your school (if they'd like their students to read this book) to teach you the things you won't learn in math or physics.

Another thing that's important to remember is that you have super skills.

We all do.

And no, that doesn't mean you can fly, or shoot spiderwebs through your fingers.

What I mean is that you have skills—things you are very, very good at. And if you develop those skills, you can become really great at something. For example, you might be skilled at drawing. If you develop that talent, you can become a great portraitist, cartoonist, or painter.

Some people don't understand this, but even simple things, such as making someone smile, is a really good skill to have.

We will look at what skills you have and how to make the most of them. And teach you the other basic skills everyone needs to know. Like tying your shoelaces. Not that we talk about shoelaces in this book, but you know, the kind of stuff that's really important.

Even if it feels boring at times.

That's why we will make it as fun as possible in this book.

Part 1: Personal Skills

CHAPTER ONE

You Have Superpowers!

Understanding what you're great at, not so great at, and the fact that you're awesome

You have superpowers.

Yep.

I'm sure of it.

But you're probably shaking your head right now, thinking that's not true. After all, you can't shoot spiderwebs with your hands or fly. You're neither Spiderman nor Superman nor Catwoman nor Wonder Woman.

Here's the thing: spiders can make spiderwebs. That's *their* superpower. Ducks can fly, that's *their* superpower. You, as a human, have other superpowers. For starters, your brain is pretty big and works well, which means you can outsmart pretty much any other animal. That's pretty cool.

But what makes YOU special? Lots of things, probably. Your parents, guardians, grandparents, friends, teachers . . . whoever is special *to you* will probably think you're super awesome.

We all have different people and animals in our lives that *we* think are special. And if you think about those special people (and animals), you can probably create a list of things you like about them. Things that you enjoy about them. Chances are, you also know what they are good at. Your cousin is great at writing stories. Your sister can make anyone laugh and is always super helpful. Your brother skates like a pro and is also very good at listening to others.

You Have Superpowers!

We all have a number of things we are good at (just as we have a number of things we are not so good at).

Some people call the things you're good at your *skill set*.

Some people are good at making other people smile or laugh.

Some people are good at math.

Some people are good at acrobatics.

Some people are good at cleaning.

Some people are good at playing baseball.

Some people are good at cooking.

Some people are good at drawing.

There are lots of different things you can be good at.

> ✓ What do you think YOU are good at? If you don't know, have a look at the chart at the end of this chapter. Perhaps an adult who knows you well can also help you fill in what you're good at.

Is your superpower not listed? Simply add it.

Does your superpower sound BORING? Cleaning doesn't sound exciting, does it? Or perhaps your superpower is building things, and you're really good at screwing in screws. Not as cool as your superhero who saves the world.

But hang on.

Do you know this woman called Marie Kondo who has become super famous for helping people tidy up their homes? She's helped millions of people live easier and happier lives.

And while screwing together things (i.e. playing around with building stuff) might not sound so cool, someone like Steve Jobs who screwed together a new laptop created a company called Apple. That company went on to become the LARGEST company in the world.

Why You Should Know Your Super Skills

Knowing what you're great at helps you when you struggle with something else. You can tell yourself "I might not be a superstar when ice skating, but I bake mean cakes." And having that confidence that you're good at something helps you stand strong when you deal with life.

Knowing what you're good at also helps when deciding which school activities you want to join, what you want to do as a career in the future, or even what hobbies to pursue.

At other times, you know you're not great at something but you LOVE doing it. You don't have to be great at art to paint. Or good at carpentry to enjoy making stuff out of wood. Some things we do just because we love doing them.

Turning Weaknesses into Strengths and Learning New Skills

You have probably noticed there are things you aren't so good at. Perhaps you struggle with getting ready on time. Perhaps math seems like a foreign language invented by aliens that's totally NOT understandable. Perhaps you're not great at skating—at least if the bruises on your bum are something to go by.

We all have things that seem to come naturally to us and things we struggle with. That's just life. The problem? Sometimes we feel really bad about the things we aren't good at. These could be things that take us longer to learn or that we never learn properly. But why do we feel bad? We aren't all natural-born soccer superstars like Lionel Messi, so why do we feel we need to be?

It seems we were all born wanting to *achieve* things. It's in our DNA. It's the force that pulls us forward. It's led to us inventing better housing (we're no longer living in huts), creating better medical care, and so forth.

So we have this drive to be great at things. That's good. So long as we don't feel bad about not being good at *everything*.

Another reason we might feel bad is because people laugh at us. But have you ever noticed that if you don't feel bad about making a mistake, but rather laugh about it, others don't care either? Even if they do laugh about it, you can laugh with them. Eventually, they start laughing *with* you instead of *at* you. If you don't take your mistakes and failures so seriously, others won't either.

And if you're ever witnessing someone messing up? Give them a helping hand!

Instead of laughing at them, tell a story about how you messed something up so they feel better.

Let's say someone falls over at the ice rink because it's their first time skating. But everyone else knows how to skate as they've grown up in parts of the world where there are cold winters.

Instead of laughing at the kid who fell over, say: "That was a really funny fall. I remember when I first learned to skate, I fell so badly I careened across the entire ice rink. My family is still laughing about it!"

You're showing the person who fell over that it's okay—it happens to everyone. And if you take their side, perhaps even help them skate, your friends are likely to follow suit.

In a sense, this is an example of how to become a great leader.

If you were the person falling over, you have a choice: laugh about it or go hide in a corner. The other kids will take a cue from you—if you aren't embarrassed, chances are they won't make a big deal out of it.

Likewise, when it comes to the things you aren't great at, you have a choice: you can either feel bad about them or you can think about what you are good at and feel good about that. What do you choose?

That said, there are some things we need to learn even if we struggle.

Let's say you struggle to be on time. To hold down a job in the future or make sure you get on a plane before it takes off, you will need to learn how to be on time.

Thankfully, you can learn how to be on time. How? You set alarms. If you need to leave home at eight, you might have to get up at seven to get ready. You can set alarms for when different things need to be done (such as getting dressed, having breakfast, brushing your teeth, and making sure your bag is packed).

Likewise, if you struggle to get your projects for school done on time, you can set deadlines for getting it done. For example, you decide which day you will do research, which day you will write the first draft, and so forth. So that the day before the project is due, you aren't standing empty-handed.

These "soft skills" such as being on time, creating good relationships, having confidence, and so forth, are things we can all work on.

What do you think are skills you aren't that great at that you should work on?

How do you think you could work at getting better at them? Ask an adult to help you, perhaps even two, so they can give you different ideas for how to get better at these things!

Also, remember that just because something isn't your super skill right now doesn't mean you won't one day become good at it. Inventor Thomas Edison struggled so much in school, his mom decided to homeschool him after a tutor called him "addled." He went on to invent the light bulb, amongst other things. He could have said "I'm bad at science" and given up, but he didn't. He also performed 1,000 experiments before he succeeded with the light bulb.

What You've Learned in This Chapter

We're not great at everything, and that's alright. We don't need to be!

There are some things we aren't great at yet, but we can try to do better.

There are some things we're really good at, and they are our super skills.

If we make a mistake, it's okay. We can laugh about it. And instead of sitting around wondering why we aren't good at that, we can choose to think about things that make us happy. Like the things we're good at!

List of Superpowers

I'm GREAT at:

- ☐ Cleaning
- ☐ Making other people smile
- ☐ Helping others with tasks
- ☐ Making others laugh
- ☐ Coming up with good jokes
- ☐ Writing stories/poetry/lyrics
- ☐ One . . . or many . . . subjects in school
- ☐ Playing a sport . . . or many different sports
- ☐ Arts and crafts (drawing, painting, working with clay/playdough, photography, crafts projects and so forth)
- ☐ Sewing, knitting, embroidery, or crocheting
- ☐ Designing things
- ☐ Looking after people, perhaps caring for them when they're sick
- ☐ Cooking
- ☐ Singing
- ☐ Doing drama
- ☐ Juggling
- ☐ Taking care of plants/gardening
- ☐ Looking after animals
- ☐ Being kind to people
- ☐ Hugging
- ☐ Swimming
- ☐ Staying calm when difficult things happen
- ☐ Playing pranks on people (so long as they are nice ones!)
- ☐ Keeping things neat and tidy
- ☐ Doing magic tricks
- ☐ Playing games (card games, online games, board games, chess, etc.)
- ☐ Doing the laundry
- ☐ Doing the dishes
- ☐ Skating
- ☐ Dancing

- ☐ Leading others (being a leader)
- ☐ Talking to people/being friendly (some people call this "the gift of the gab")
- ☐ Making friends
- ☐ Speaking different languages
- ☐ Planning
- ☐ Organizing
- ☐ Carpentry
- ☐ Plumbing
- ☐ Building things
- ☐ Coming up with cool ideas
- ☐ Memorizing things
- ☐ Thinking outside the box
- ☐ Mechanics
- ☐ Making others feel loved
- ☐ Making music
- ☐ Seeing things in a positive light (when something bad happens, you always find something good in the situation)
- ☐ Handling money (budgeting, saving, and so forth)
- ☐ Being on time
- ☐ Baking
- ☐ Blending perfumes
- ☐ Making jewelry
- ☐ Please add any other SUPER SKILLS you might have! There are many more out there!

_____

_____

_____

_____

CHAPTER TWO

Why Do You Feel and Act This Way?

You have the power to change your actions and reactions

You're playing a soccer match against another team. You're really amped up about it. Your teammates are excited. Your parents and friends are rooting for you. You feel great.

Then your team loses. Now you feel bad. Why is that? You lost, sure, but that's not why you feel bad.

Wait. Say that again?

The reason you feel bad (sad, down, whatever you want to call it) isn't because you lost the game. It's because of what you think about losing the game.

Let's rewind a bit.

Let's say yes, you lost the game, but you walked out of there thinking, "Man, I had so much fun playing today and while we lost, I learned that there are things our team needs to improve on. If we do that, we can win so many more matches!"

Here's a secret: it's not what happens to us but how we see it that determines how we feel.

A Positive Attitude Equals a Positive Experience

In a sense, we write little stories about the events we experience. And what we make up in our story determines how we feel.

What are some events that happened in your life that made you feel not so good? Perhaps they made you angry. Perhaps they made you sad. Perhaps they made you feel unloved.

Now, looking at those events (preferably with an adult), how could you see them differently?

Let's say you are failing in math and you feel bad about it. Let's say instead, that you think that even though you're failing, it won't stop you. You will learn more, and one day, you will have the career you want, even if you'll never be great at math.

Sometimes it's relatively small stuff that gets us down.

Sometimes it's big stuff. Like losing a friend, someone passing away, or having to move to a new place. That's when we have to be really clever about the stories we create around it.

Let's say you're moving. You're leaving your grandparents *and* your best friend behind. You're going to an unknown, scary-looking, big city.

That's a *good* reason to be sad. It's also a *good* reason to be happy.

Let's create a new story about moving.

"I'm going to move with my parents to a new city. It's exciting—I'm going to see places I've never seen before. There are candy stores, cinemas, sports centers, parks, and lots of other cool places that I will get to visit. I will meet a whole bunch of new people who I can make friends with. I'm a bit shy, so I'm going to ask at the new school about some extracurricular activities I can do where I get to meet people in small groups and where a teacher can help introduce me. I will miss my best friend and grandparents, but I will be coming back for epic sleepovers. I'm still a bit nervous, but I have asked my parents to help me find exercises that help me be braver so I can enjoy this adventure more. I can't wait to make new memories in a new place!"

And here's an important thing: if you're happy and confident when you arrive in the new city, do you think it'll be easier to make new friends? Come up with fun things to do? Enjoy the new city?

Of course it will.

Your attitude determines not just how you feel but the *reactions* others have to you.

Just imagine this: a child at school goes up to the front of the classroom to do a presentation. He's looking down. His shoulders are hunched over. He says nervously, "I don't think this will be any good." Then he mumbles and stumbles his way through the presentation.

Imagine instead: the same child goes up to the front of the classroom, shrugs his shoulders, and laughs, saying, "I'm not sure I'm good at presentations, but I'll give it a shot. Don't be too harsh on me, okay?" Then he looks out at the students and speaks to them confidently as he presents what he has to say. His voice is loud enough to be heard and, when at one point he forgets what to say, or makes a mistake, he laughs, looks at his notes, and then keeps going.

Do you think the audience will react differently in these different scenarios? They will, right? Because people react differently depending on how *you* act. It's the same child. He's just presenting himself differently. His *attitude* is different.

Plus, your attitude determines what *you* do. If you're sad about being in a new place, you might sit looking at pictures of your old home and sulk because of how much you miss it. But if you're excited, you might be googling cool things to do and then going out and doing them.

That doesn't mean everything will go right. It just means you'll be actively looking for the good stuff and find more of it. It also means that when bad things happen, you feel better as you ask yourself what stories you're writing about them.

If you do mess up a presentation, it doesn't mean you're bad at giving presentations.

It doesn't mean no one likes you because they booed you.

It doesn't mean tomorrow will be a bad day.

It means you gave one bad presentation around kids with a bad attitude.

So next time something happens that makes you feel down, will you let it ruin your day or will you rewrite the story and help yourself feel better?

The Pause Button: Thinking Before You Act

People often joke that humans are a bit like robots. But is it true? Do we sometimes act like we've been "programmed" to act? Well, sort of. If we get used to doing something one way, we tend to keep doing it the same way. Like, you wouldn't think to make yourself a cup of hot chocolate while standing upside down, would you?

Alright, that's illogical. But I bet you use the same tools and gestures to make the hot chocolate that you normally do.

Another way of putting it is saying we're creatures of habit. If you easily get angry, you continue to easily get angry unless you decide to change.

Ah, *if* you decide to change.

But how do you change?

If you always get angry when your brother is annoying or when you're told you have to go to bed, how do you stop getting angry? Or if you always get nervous when doing presentations in school, how do you stop getting nervous?

You create a mind movie.

Say what?

Well, I call it a mind movie because it's like a movie you see in your mind.

Let's say you *do* get nervous when doing presentations. For a week before your next presentation, you spend time every day imagining giving the presentation. But you imagine giving the presentation confidently.

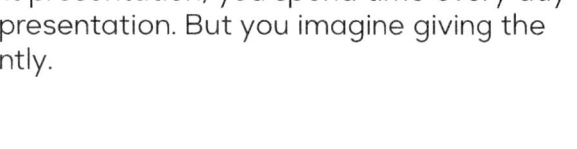

Here's how you do it:

> Close your eyes.
>
> Now imagine standing in your classroom. What can you see? Smell? Hear?
>
> And how do you feel? You feel nervous.
>
> Okay, acknowledge that. It's alright. Don't push it away. Just sit with it for a moment or two. Your feelings are okay. They aren't there to harm you, just alert you to the fact that something is up—whether good or bad.
>
> Now, imagine feeling different. Imagine feeling powerful. Happy. Confident. Imagine that everyone in the room is *wanting* to hear you speak.
>
> Yes, the audience wants you to succeed. They want to listen to something that's engaging, fun, and interesting.
>
> Then, imagine speaking in an easy and engaging way. Imagine how simple that can be. Words just flow out of your mouth. The right words come to you easy as pie.

If you imagine that for a week, chances are when you do your presentation, you feel a lot more confident. As a result, the audience will be a lot more engaged and less likely to boo you out (because sad as it is, there's always someone looking to put others down).

Athletes do this all the time—they imagine what it will be like hitting the ball at the perfect angle or running faster than they ever have before.

And here's the fascinating part: studies have shown that "rehearsing in your mind" brings on real-world results. People who sit thinking about throwing a basketball into a hoop every day get better at it! They improve almost as much as people who are out only practicing for the same amount of time every day.

Why Do You Feel and Act This Way?

Your mind is powerful. That's why it's so important to feed it with the right information and get a hold of it when it's going off in the wrong direction. Such as when it starts painting horrible scenarios about you doing a bad presentation, losing a soccer game, or falling off a horse or your bike.

When you have those moments of panic where you imagine everything going wrong (and we all have them), simply stop and imagine them going right! And set aside some time every day to do this—preferably at night before going to bed and first thing in the morning.

Now, if you're doing a presentation, you can obviously rehearse the presentation out loud. But start with doing it in your mind first, so you get a feeling of how you want to *feel*. Then you can learn the words while feeling that way.

Let's say you always get annoyed with your brother for taking your things without asking and start screaming at him (making him angry which leads to a fight). Imagine over and over again how you want to react the next time you get annoyed. Perhaps you want to walk away? Perhaps you want to ask him kindly not to keep taking your things. Perhaps you want to call a parent to deal with it.

Whatever it is, imagine what you will do and how it will make you feel. You have to do it over and over again. Change takes time.

Perhaps you want to hit the ball perfectly when playing baseball. Then you practice this in your mind over and over again.

Basically, you create a movie in your mind about what you want to do and how you want to feel when doing it.

This is perhaps especially important if you already made a mistake.

For example, you messed up a dance performance. You come home. You see what happened over and over again in your mind.

Actually, this happened to me. I performed with my dance class in school once, but they'd put wires across the stage. So we all stumbled. It was a disaster. And I replayed it over and over again in my mind.

Thankfully, I also replayed over and over again in my mind how much fun I had connecting with the other artists backstage. It didn't put me off performing.

But it could have, had I not loved dancing so much and already known I was pretty good at it.

What you can do when things go wrong is go back and replay the movie. What would you have liked to have happened? By doing this, you are more likely to get it right next time.

You will probably also feel better about it.

Remember the stories we tell ourselves? Even if you get something wrong, make up a good story about it!

And this isn't just about things we do. It can be things that happen to you. Such as someone dying. If your dog passes away, you can tell yourself that's it—you'll never have a furry friend again. Or you can tell yourself that thanks to your dog, you've discovered how wonderful dogs are. Your dog taught you many things, and you had wonderful times together. Thanks to that, you know dogs will always be in your life. You will go on to make many other pups happy by spending time with them. You will always miss and remember your first dog, and in his/her honor, you will continue to love dogs and make them happy.

When you get sad about your dog, you can remind yourself of this story and play it like a movie in your mind, imagining how happy your dog would be to know you're making new dog friends.

But what if creating a mind movie isn't working? What if you just can't stop feeling nervous when rehearsing your presentation? What if you still feel petrified at the thought of meeting new people? What if having to go to school still makes you feel bored?

Then it's time for your super alter ego to come out.

Your Super Alter Ego: Becoming Your Inner Hero

Todd Herman wrote a book called *The Alter Ego Effect* after having coached some of the world's top athletes and celebrities.

So what did he do for these famous people?

He taught them how to be other people.

Uh, come again?

Todd taught them to pretend to be someone else when doing tasks that they felt nervous about.

Saying he taught them to be someone else is perhaps not quite right. But they tapped into another persona.

Let's say you don't like going to the doctors. So next time you go to the doctors, you want to be brave. You then decide you have a superpower: being brave. Who is someone you know who is brave? Perhaps it's Superman. Perhaps it's a lion tamer. Perhaps it's your mom or dad. Next time you go to the doctors, you pretend to be them.

Truly it's you being brave. Anyone can be brave. But pretending to be someone else—or imitating them—can help us tap into that side of ourselves.

Maybe you're not so great at writing tests; they make you nervous. So next time you write a test, you pretend to be as cool as Catwoman when you sit down to write.

If you get stressed when playing soccer, you pretend to have the confidence of Messi as you walk onto the soccer field.

If you freak out whenever you make a mistake, you pretend to be a comedian you like and laugh it off. The comedian thinks mistakes are funny. That's all there is to it.

If you've never before enjoyed learning, pretend to be a super geek with incredible brain powers who loves to learn.

You, so to speak, try to walk in someone else's shoes and see the world through their eyes.

Basically, you create a persona—it could be a superhero, a character in a movie, or someone you know—who has the traits you need.

So if you need to be calmer, who do you know stays cool as a cucumber no matter what is going on around them?

If you need to be braver, who do you know is brave?

Sometimes, by pretending we're someone else, we can improve our own traits. After you've done this for a while, you will probably realize that you now have the new trait. You no longer have to pretend to be someone else.

You can also choose an object that helps transform you into this character. Perhaps a special ring can help you feel like a princess. Or a pair of sunglasses can turn you into a superhero. Kind of like how Clark Kent is only Clark Kent until he changes into his Superman outfit.

At the same time, Superman *is* Clark Kent. It's just that the "super side" of his persona comes out.

In a similar way, you can imagine having superpowers and create your own superhero who you turn into when you need to.

When It's Time to Get Support or Change Your Life

In this chapter, we've covered how you can change your *reactions* to events and how you can write your own stories about what is happening.

Someone bullying you doesn't *mean* you're not good enough. Most of the time it *means* the bully is feeling insecure and feels better when putting other people down. It's not about

Why Do You Feel and Act This Way?

YOU. It's about THEM. Having decided to view it that way, you *feel* differently about it and *act* differently.

That said, unless it's someone just teasing you once or twice and then changing their attitude, you have to do something about it.

You should NEVER have to face bullies alone.

Speak with teachers and your parents/guardians. The school should be able to tell your parents what they will do to help make the bullying stop. If it doesn't, speak with your parents about getting more people involved. For some kids, this could mean going to another school. You might also want other support. Therapists, counselors, and psychologists, as well as life coaches, help people build confidence and teach them skills like how to handle the kind of emotions you might feel if you have been bullied.

This isn't just about bullies in school.

It could be a teacher or other adult being mean to you.

Or it could be something going on in your life that you really don't like.

Let's say you've started a new school. You've told yourself great stories about going there. You've asked adults for support with what you struggle with. But the school focuses on art or PE and it's just not the school for you as you're into academics or science.

Then you need to speak up—talk to an adult that can help you.

Or, perhaps, your parents enrolled you in a soccer club, but no matter how hard you try to enjoy soccer, you know in your heart of hearts that it's swimming you want to do. Or join the scouts. Then you have to speak with some adults about it. If you're uncomfortable approaching your parents, then speak to your grandparents or another adult that can talk to them.

Having support in the form of teachers, parents, and professionals, like therapists, can help you build superpowers faster!

What You've Learned in This Chapter

You learned that you make up stories about everything that happens to you. If you change the story, you feel different about what happens. This shapes your attitude. That, in turn, affects what you do and how others view you.

Remember the example of losing a soccer game?

You can either tell yourself a story about what a failure you are and feel defeated or tell a story about how much fun you had playing, how much you've learned, and what you will do differently. As you feel happy, you might choose to celebrate and have fun, instead of staying at home and feeling sad. People will also react to you differently if you show up sad and feeling like you've failed or happy and feeling like you've learned something new.

Your feelings aren't bad—even if they feel bad. They are simply there to alert you about something. You need to pay attention to them. If you feel good or bad, why is that? What are you seeing in your mind that creates those feelings?

We all create mind movies when we think about the future, whether we realize it or not. If we feel bad about an upcoming presentation, it's because we imagine it going badly.

We can change our mind movie. This is also how we change knee-jerk reactions, such as always shouting at a sibling when they're annoying.

To create a mind movie, simply sit down and acknowledge how you feel about something right now—such as getting angry with your sibling or getting nervous about a presentation. Then imagine it how

Why Do You Feel and Act This Way?

you want it to be instead. Imagine yourself calmly dealing with your sibling. Imagine yourself giving a great presentation.

We don't change overnight. For this to work, you have to imagine it several times.

A good habit is to sit down to imagine things—every night before you sleep and in the morning. Consider how you feel about the day ahead. Then imagine how you want the day to unfold and how you want to feel and act in different situations.

If you find it difficult to imagine doing things differently or feeling differently about something, you can imagine stepping into a super persona—an alter ego. You can make up this super persona, or you can think of someone you know who has the superpower you need and pretend to be them while you tackle whatever it is you have some issues with.

CHAPTER THREE

Navigating Change and Loss

In life, nothing ever remains the same—that's why it's an adventure. But how do we deal with change that feels really bad?

The good thing about life?

Things always change.

That means life is an adventure.

For example, today it's raining and you don't know what to do. You feel bored. Tomorrow you meet a new boy called Tim at school. He teaches you how to build marble runs that are so complicated it's like magic. The next day, you bring Tim home with you after school for a visit. It's raining. But now it's fun because you're building marble runs.

Just because we're bored today, doesn't mean we will be bored tomorrow.

Just because we're in pain today, or feeling sick today, doesn't mean we'll be in pain or feel sick tomorrow.

Another sad thing? Just because we're friends with someone today, doesn't mean we will be friends with them tomorrow.

As people grow up, they change. Even when they're adults, they change. Things happen to us in life, and we learn new things and become different people.

Think of it this way. Let's say Jenny grew up in a poor neighborhood. Her parents weren't very nice to her. She had no food at home. So she started stealing. When Jenny is in her teens, she gets caught by the police for shoplifting several times and is sent to juvenile prison (juvvie). At juvvie, Jenny finally gets enough food to eat. She gets teachers who teach her to love and like herself. They pay attention to her and help her understand life better.

When Jenny leaves juvvie, she's placed in a nice foster home. The family cares about her and helps her with school. Jenny goes on to study at college and becomes a teacher. When she goes back to the area where she grew up, people don't recognize her. She's not the same person. Nor does she want to be friends with the people she grew up with who are still stealing.

People change. For better or for worse.

And as we change, we sometimes change our friends. Jenny doesn't want to be friends with her old friends because they aren't living the fulfilled life she's now living.

Other times, it's not so clear cut.

Some kids grow up riding and loving horses, but as they reach their teens, they don't enjoy it so much anymore. Maybe they prefer listening to music or dancing. Suddenly they become really into clothes, too. And the friends they grew up with who still love horses and being in nature just don't seem like people they can connect with anymore.

Parents might also fall out of love and split up or have a divorce even if they love one another as friends.

Other couples love each other, but they are not good at building happy relationships. They split up because of that.

Other people split up because one person has a problem with alcohol, or their finances, or something else and won't deal with it and it affects the family negatively.

What I'm saying is that friends and partners don't always last for life.

The good thing? Even if it hurts when something comes to an end, you have the opportunity to make new friends and find new partners.

The difficult thing? When something just ends, it's hard not to think about it. And when we think about it, we get sad. We just can't imagine being friends or being in a relationship with anyone else.

People are often like that. They find change difficult.

It's not always about losing people, either. It could be moving to a new home. A new school. A new city.

It could be losing a toy we love or an animal we love.

When things change, we mourn what we lost. We long to go back to what we had.

So how do we deal with this?

What Is Grief and How Do You Overcome It?

When we lose something, or someone, sometimes we don't want to accept it. We wonder what would happen if only? We think if our parents divorce, they will get back together. If someone dies, it's a mistake, and really, it was someone else in the hospital bed. If our friend says they no longer want to be our friend, they will change their mind. We hold on to a dream of things going back to what they were.

The problem with that? We don't really face the fact, feel the pain, and move on with our lives.

Those might be some big words.

Imagine if your friend says she no longer wants to be your friend. You think she'll change her mind. You daydream about that. It hurts less that way.

But your friend does not come back. She gets new friends. And it hurts every time she does. If you accept that your friend isn't coming back, it will hurt.

When it hurts, you have to say, "Alright, I know it will hurt. I know it will go away. I can feel the hurt. Now I will go and do something else, that will take my mind off it and that will make me feel good."

When the pain hits, when we cry, it seems impossible that we will feel better, but WE WILL.

We have to make a decision to do something that makes us feel better, even if we don't feel like it.

When you are tired, you don't feel like getting out of bed. When you're grieving, you don't feel like going and having some fun.

We have to push ourselves to do what we don't want to. By doing that, we start to feel better.

A tip is to tell your parents/guardian how you are feeling and ask them to help you. Tell them you need help to do things you like. And ask if you can tell them when you're sad and they can help push you to do some nice things. And give you a hug. Because hugs also make us feel good.

You can't push the pain away. When it comes, you have to say, "Alright, I feel it. I will feel it for one minute and let it wash over me. Then I'm going to focus on things that will make me feel good."

Grief can be so bad sometimes we don't feel anything at all for some time (you can slip into something called depression). We don't feel happy when we do the things we love. But if we keep at it, slowly our joy returns.

Once you accept something, you can also decide what mind movie you want to create now.

If your friend is gone, you can decide to do activities where you meet other people. That can lead to you making new friends.

If you're shy, you can decide to watch videos online on how to be more confident and ask someone, like a parent, to come with you and do things where you meet other people. Sometimes, we need a bit of help.

If your parents get a divorce, you can't get them back under the same roof. But you can decide you want to have good relationships with both of them and work on that. You can work on creating nice rooms in their different homes. On having as much fun as possible when you see either one of them.

If you don't accept your parents' divorce, you will either daydream of them getting back together or be really angry. Perhaps you'll sit alone in your room and sulk whenever you go to their places. But will that make you happy? Will it make them happy? Will it lead to fun experiences?

You can go back to Chapter Two and have a look at the way we create stories about things in our lives. What story are you creating about what happened? What story would you love to create?

What's on the "Other Side"?

I was with my grandma in the hospice when she passed away. There, they gave me a little book saying that when someone comes to the end of their life, they go on a journey we cannot follow. It's like watching a ship sail off into the horizon—the ship gets smaller and smaller until it disappears.

People have different ideas about what happens after death. Some say it's like going to sleep forever. Some say you go to Heaven. Some think you become a spirit roaming the Earth. Some think you are born again as someone else but keep the same soul—that the soul is immortal.

Many people who have died and come back to life—such as when your heart stops and someone performs CPR and it starts beating again—say they saw other people who have passed away when they were "on the other side."

Your parents might believe a certain thing and explain it to you.

The important thing to remember is that it's like watching a ship sail away—we need to say goodbye and wish the other person a nice journey. Where they're going, we can't go. Not now. But we can still hope that they will feel happy and have fun where they are going! Just because they are no longer here with us, doesn't mean we have to be sad for them. They are someplace else now.

Living and Loving

When people die, we often feel like we *should* be sad. We might even feel guilty for being alive. Why do we get to live when someone else doesn't?

We don't know why. We just know that everyone dies eventually. And the people who loved us when they were alive would want us to be happy. They've gone somewhere else, but they want us to be happy here. They would not want us to be sad. They'd want us to enjoy our lives as much as possible.

> *If you love people, you want them to be happy. Therefore, the best thing you can do for whoever passed away is to live life as much as possible. Have fun. Go on adventures. Treasure the people in your life.*
>
> *Think of life as a gift. We all get the same gift. How long it lasts varies. But we can all look after it, treasure it, and use it as best as possible.*

Many people also feel guilty if they start loving other people after someone in their life died. If you lose your mom, you might feel like you shouldn't replace her.

You won't. Your mother will always be your mother. That doesn't mean you can't love other women who are like mothers to you.

Your mother wouldn't want you to grow up alone. She'd want you to be loved. To get guidance from other women. She'd want you to have everything she gave you and more.

The women in your life that might "mother" you will be different from your mom. You will love them differently, but it doesn't mean you'll love them *less*.

That's the thing—everyone's different. We love them for different reasons, but we love them all.

When my mom died, my grandmothers helped raise me. They were different from my mom, but I loved them both. I still missed my mom, but I let my grandmothers love and care for me. I needed that love and care. Just like you need love and care from someone if you've lost a person in your life.

If we are open to love, there will always be love in our lives. It just looks different with different people. We will always miss the people we lose, but it shouldn't stop us from enjoying the other people in our lives. And love them. Because those people also need love.

And if the person you lost is out there somewhere, they will be very happy to see you happy. So try to stay open and let others in instead of hiding away, even if you're in pain. It hurts to lose people, but we can heal.

There's so much love out there, don't miss out on it.

Things You Can Do to Get Through Grief

When we lose someone, it can be difficult. Sometimes, it helps to talk to people. We can talk to the people close to us, like a relative or friend. We can also talk to therapists who are good at helping people going through mourning. They can help give us tips on how to feel better again.

It's also important to do the things we love, even when we don't feel like it.

Truth be told, we usually feel like doing *nothing* when we are sad.

So, either we force ourselves to do something, or we ask others to help us. For example, you might ask a friend or relative to help ensure you still show up for your favorite activities.

Here are some things that might help you feel better:

- Spending time in nature (and spending time outdoors every day, even if it's not in nature)
- Playing outdoors with friends
- Exercise

- Listening to calming or happy music
- Watching comedies
- Reading funny books
- Spending time with friends and family
- Eating healthy foods
- Making things with our hands, like doing art, crafts, and carpentry
- Partaking in activities we love, whether it be horse riding or meeting with friends to play board games
- Going for swims in the sea or lake or having cold baths or showers (with an adult when it's safe and only if you don't have a heart condition)
- Getting enough sleep at regular hours

All of the above makes our brain release chemicals that make us feel better. So even if you don't *feel* like doing them, you'll feel better *after* you do them. You might have to keep going for quite a while to truly feel better, so don't give up!

And remember, the person, or persons, you lost would want you to be happy. They know you miss them. They know you love them. They also want to know you're happy and loved.

What You've Learned in This Chapter

When things change, we sometimes hold on to what used to be. We daydream about things going back to being like they were. We might refuse to accept that things have changed.

But it's only when we accept that things have changed that we can create beautiful experiences in life as it is *now*. We might not get our friend back, have our parents remarry, or something like that, but we can make new friends and be happy with our parents as things are now.

When things change or we lose someone we love, we often feel sad. We need to feel sad, but we also have to push ourselves to do the things we love so that we feel better. Sometimes that's hard, just like it's hard getting out of bed when we're tired. We don't feel like it. We still have to do it and keep doing it until we start feeling good again.

If someone we love passes away, we sometimes feel guilty for being alive and having fun. We shouldn't. Because the person we lost would want us to be happy.

If we lose a parent or someone else close to us, we might also feel guilty for "replacing" them. We shouldn't be. We still miss that special person. They were unique. We will always miss them. But there's plenty of space in our hearts for new people. They will be different from the person we lost. We will love them for different things, but we will still love them. And that we can love so many different people is part of what makes life beautiful.

CHAPTER FOUR

Making Super Decisions

You've already learned a bit about why you react the way you do, now how can you learn to make the decisions you need to make to create a super awesome life?

You are shy, so you don't like being around lots of people. So when someone asks you to come to a party, you say no.

Now, imagine going to that party and having lots of fun. Making new friends.

Would you still say no?

Let's say instead that, when you're old enough to vote, someone asks you to vote for a specific person as the next President or Prime Minister. Who would you vote for? Is that because someone else told you they were great? Or because you did the research and found out lots of good things about them?

When we make decisions, we have to ask ourselves why we are making them.

You're one day going to have to decide if you're going to the party you've just been invited to, or not.

You're also going to have to decide which President/Prime Minister you're voting for.

There are a ton of other decisions that have to be made. You have to decide what career you want. Where you want to live. If you want to go to college/university. If you want to spend your savings on a bike or keep saving for something else.

So how do we make good decisions?

Here are some things you can ask yourself when making decisions that will help you along.

1. Are you doing or not doing something because you're scared? Or because it's what you truly want/don't want to do?
2. Are you doing/not doing something because someone else told you to do/not do it? If so, was the person who told you to do it or not do it a good person to ask? Do they know a lot about the topic? And are they unbiased (are they 100% fair)?
3. Have you educated yourself about it? For example, if you want to go to a camp this summer, have you researched that camp and other camps and decided it's the best camp?
4. Are there any risks involved? If you decide to go rock climbing, for example, are there any risks involved? Can you mitigate those risks (i.e. make them smaller by, in this example, using safety gear)? Is it still worth doing it with the risks involved?
5. If you're asking other people for advice about some decision you have to make, ask yourself if they are educated about it. And if they are biased or unbiased. Sometimes it helps getting different opinions, too.

These days people talk a lot about "fake news" as lots of people post things on social media that aren't true. People who know nothing about medicine give medical advice. People who know nothing about investments give investment advice.

That's why you have to question information. Who wrote it? Are they educated? Are they biased? Only when you know that can you make a decision whether to use the information or not.

The Super Skill of Making Good Decisions

Let's say you have to make a decision about summer camp.

Your friend is super excited about going to a surf camp.

You'd love to spend more time with your friend. And you've heard the camp they're going to is AWESOME. But you aren't that interested in surfing.

The two other camps you've heard of seem to have better activities, but while the rumor is that the camps are alright, no one is saying they're AWESOME. And your friend isn't going to them.

So what should you do?

You have to do some research to find out if these are the only camps available. Then you have to decide what's the most important thing to you. Perhaps it's doing what you love most. Perhaps it's being at a camp where the atmosphere is amazing. Perhaps it's being with your friend.

Here's a process you can follow to really think through and make a good decision:

1. Look up information: find out more about the camps you know of, and see if you can find another camp that seems to be AWESOME *and* have the activities you'd love to participate in

2. List the pros and cons (i.e. the good and bad stuff) about the different camps (including any potential risks and how much it would cost)

3. Talk through the pros and cons with an unbiased adult (i.e. not your teacher who absolutely wants you to go to the camp they once went to no matter how you feel about it)

4. Once you've narrowed down the list to two or three camps, make up a mind movie about the different choices, imagining the worst and best case scenarios. That can help you figure out what makes you the most excited and ensure you're not avoiding something just because you are scared

5. Now, which is the camp you choose? And what experiences would you like to create once you're there?

By the way, you remember mind movies, right? It's when you close your eyes and imagine something. In this case, you close your eyes and imagine being at a camp. Like what it will truly be like being there, as you walk around the grounds and interact with the other kids at the camp.

Know that just because we imagine something being one way or another, it doesn't always end up that way.

Let's say you chose one camp because they offer tennis classes. You get there, and yes, there are tennis classes but you don't like the teacher.

Could you still have a nice time?

Yes. You could decide that you don't care if you don't like the teacher; you're there to learn and have fun with new people.

Or you can decide to think about how annoying the teacher is and have an awful experience.

This is why you should know upfront what you want out of an experience. That way, even if things don't go your way, you can take a step back, remember what you wanted out of it, and then focus on achieving it even if the circumstances aren't ideal.

Let's say instead that your friend is having a party. You thought about it beforehand and imagined how it would be—lots of fun things happening that you get to share with your friends. But the people you thought would come aren't there. The activities you thought you'd do aren't happening. The party seems dull. Can you still create something fun? Can you still connect with some of the people there?

Yes.

You just always have to remember what it is you *want out of a situation*. Don't lose track of it just because things aren't going as planned.

Instead, turn things around.

> Jack was starting high school next year. Only, where he lived, he had to choose between different high schools.
>
> One school was a bit further away, offered great teachers, and was a pretty big school with lots of kids from all over. They were also known for having good sports teams.

The other school was smaller but had a beautiful garden and great sports facilities. It was also closer.

Jack was excited about the school with great teachers and good sports teams as he was hoping to do swimming and perhaps even get a scholarship to college. But he didn't like the fact that he had to travel farther to get there. And he was scared of meeting so many new kids at once, even if it was exciting, too. Plus, the school building was kind of ugly. He didn't really feel like the school was welcoming.

The smaller school was easy to get to, he knew most of the kids he'd attend school with, and it was a beautiful school that felt very welcoming.

Jack felt that the easy thing would just be to attend the nearby school. He told his mother he was unsure what to choose.

"List the pros and cons of each school," she told him.

Jack did that. "I still don't know."

"Close your eyes and imagine being at either school. Imagine the best and worst case scenario for each one."

Jack did that.

"Alright, what did you imagine it'd be like?" his mom asked.

"Well, with the small school, I first imagined it'd be fun to be with my friends. And I love the building and the sports facilities there. But then I imagined I'd be sad if I didn't get as good sports coaching as at the other school and didn't get a scholarship to college. And that I would always be upset if I didn't dare try the bigger school."

"And what did you imagine for the big school?"

"Well, first I imagined the bad stuff. What it would be like on the first day before knowing anyone. And how bored I'd be when traveling there. Then, I imagined being in class with good teachers and being introduced to lots of people and having wonderful swimming classes. I imagined listening to music and audiobooks on my way to school and even doing homework on the bus."

"And if you went with the best case scenario, where would you like to go?"

"To the big school. But what if I end up not liking it?"

"Then you can always change schools. Better yet, perhaps you can schedule a tour there and see what it's like before you make your mind up?"

"That's a great idea, Mom!"

Jack realized that had he made a decision right away, he'd probably chosen the small school because it felt safer somehow. But if it went well at the big school, he'd probably enjoy it more and more easily get into the college of his dreams.

What You've Learned in This Chapter

What's the formula for making a good decision?

Well, unlike math, there isn't really a formula.

BUT there is a process you can try out:

1. Learn a little bit about your choices (if it's something you can look up in a book or online).
2. List the pros and cons (the good and bad stuff) of the different options you have, including any potential risks and how to mitigate them (i.e. make them smaller).
3. Speak with a couple of (unbiased) adults about your pros and cons.
4. Close your eyes and make up a movie in your mind about the best and worst thing that could happen with either choice (perhaps talk to an adult about it to see what they have to say).
5. Choose what it is you'd like to create and think about how to go about creating that!

CHAPTER FIVE

Setting Goals to Achieve Your Dreams

What are goals? Why are they important? How do you set goals and nail them?

A goal is something you decide you want to achieve.

For example, your goal might be to do twenty push-ups a day. Or it might be to become an actress. Or a millionaire.

Some goals are short-term goals, such as wanting to cook a nice dinner today. Other goals are long-term, such as wanting to become fit, or becoming a plumber.

If you have a big goal, you usually have to break it down into smaller goals.

If you want to get strong and fit, you have to work out what you need to do every week or every day to get that fitness level, like how and what you will eat and strength training.

If you want to become an actress, you have to work out what to do to become an actress, such as trying out different acting classes, joining the theater group in school, going to a theater camp, reading books about different acting techniques, learning to use your voice, and so forth.

> ❝ Goals are good because they tend to motivate us and fill us with purpose. And breaking them down can help us understand what we need to do to get where we want to be. We can also measure them—see that we tick off different goals every day. ❞

Setting Goals to Achieve Your Dreams

🎯 The Difference Between Goals and Dreams

A long time ago, my principal told me there was a difference between a dream and a goal. A dream is just a dream. A goal is something you move towards.

Let's look at a story about two girls who wanted to become vets to show you what the difference between dreams and goals are.

> Mary lived on a farm. She loved waking up early and spending time in the stables, helping to muck out and feed the horses and cows.
>
> When Mary came home from school every day, she'd help her mother feed the chickens and take care of the vegetable patch. Mary truly loved farm life.
>
> Mary went to school in town, and her best friend was Lisa.
>
> Lisa lived in a big apartment building in the city and had never spent much time with animals, but she thought they were really cute. And she liked Mary's dogs.

Mary told Lisa she wanted to become a vet so she could help animals. Lisa said that was fantastic and perhaps she could become one too. After all, the two of them used to watch YouTube videos of vets rescuing stray dogs. It seemed like a fun job to have.

When Lisa told her this, Mary looked thoughtful. "I think," she said, "that perhaps you need to actually see what a vet does before you decide."

"But a vet helps animals, I know that," Lisa protested.

"Yes, but do you know what it's like helping animals?" Mary asked.

"Well, you help them!" Lisa said.

Mary told her, "One of my mom's friends is a vet, and I think you should meet her."

A few days later, Mary and Lisa went to see Dr. Frida.

"This is so exciting!" Lisa exclaimed as Frida showed her around her practice. "But what's that smell?"

"It's disinfectant. We have to disinfect all surfaces so that there's no bacteria when we work with wounded animals. Come, why don't you accompany me as I see some patients today?"

"Sure," both girls said happily.

The first patient was Max, a Golden Retriever pup who'd injured his paw by stepping on a thorn.

"Oh, he's so cute," Lisa said.

"He sure is," Frida replied.

All that Frida needed to do for Max was remove the thorn and put on a bandage. "He will be right as rain in no time," Frida said.

"Wow," Lisa exclaimed, "it's so nice to see you help animals."

The next patient was really different. It was a cat called Molly who had torn open a big gash and blood was flowing from the wound.

"Oh," Lisa mumbled, then sat down as she got dizzy from the sight of blood.

"Are you alright?" Mary asked her.

"Yes, but I feel a bit faint."

"I should have warned you," Frida exclaimed. "I thought you knew you weren't sensitive because you chose to come here today, but I should have said something."

Mary helped Lisa sit down, then watched as Frida stitched up the wound on the cat after first giving it a local anesthetic. A very happy "cat mama" received her cat back.

"Thank you," she said, tears in her eyes. "I was scared I was going to lose Molly today. You did an excellent job with her."

"She should heal just fine given the wound doesn't become infected."

After Molly and her cat mama left, Frida got a phone call and turned to the girls. "It's time for a home visit! We're going to help a foal into the world. There seems to be some complications so Mr. Collins wants me there to make sure everything goes smoothly."

After that, they had lunch before they saw some animals for routine checkups and minor injuries. Then, someone rushed in carrying a dog that had been in a car accident. Lisa immediately turned away as she still felt nauseous at the sight of blood.

"I'm so sorry," Frida told the owner after examining the dog, "but there is nothing I can do for him. It'd be better to put him to sleep. No matter what I do, he won't survive. By putting him to sleep, you can save him the pain."

At this, Lisa started crying and decided to leave the room.

"Are you alright?" Mary asked, following her friend out.

"No. I could never work here. That poor dog won't survive."

"I know, but Frida is helping so many other animals. If she hadn't helped that cat earlier, she wouldn't have survived either. And at least now, the dog won't be in pain."

"I get that, and it's beautiful to see, but I can't handle the bad cases. I just want to cry now. And all that blood earlier, I don't think it's for me."

"You know you can learn to handle seeing blood, right? At least I think you can."

"Still, I just don't think I could handle seeing injured animals ALL day long. It's hard."

"I guess I got used to being around animals early on. I saw births at the farm that went well and births that went wrong. I saw some animals dying and others being healed. And I wanted to help heal as many as possible."

"That's great, I'm happy there are people like you and Frida. I just think I need to find a profession that does not involve injuries. And I've never thought about how smelly animals or disinfectants are either. I'm not sure I could be around such strong smells all day long."

Mary smiled. "That's why I wanted you to come here. So you can see what it's really like being a vet. I just had a feeling that maybe there was something else that you would love *more*."

"There must be. Now I just have to find it. What do you think about becoming a chef? I always loved cooking."

"Well, I guess we could find a chef and ask to come see what it's like."

"Great idea."

And with that decision made, the girls go on an adventure to find out what profession will truly suit Lisa.

Lisa had a dream of becoming a vet, but it was just a dream—she didn't really know what becoming a vet meant. She wanted to help animals, but she could adopt a stray dog, cat, or other animal if that's all she wanted to do.

A true goal is something you understand and then take action to achieve.

Another way of saying it is that all goals are dreams, but not all dreams are goals.

Did you get that? Otherwise, take a moment to think on it or ask an adult!

Dream Big: Getting Going with Goals

Now, as with the example in the story, let's say you think you want to become a vet, but you don't really know what the day-to-day life of a vet is like. So the first thing you have to do is figure out what it's like. Perhaps, you can find some YouTube videos or documentaries about it. Because those videos you've been watching about saving cute pups on the street aren't really realistic in describing the day-to-day life of a vet.

For example, as a vet, you might need to give animals injections. Perform surgeries. Help with delivering little ones. You would spend time in stables, with angry animals, with badly wounded animals, and so forth. That's, possibly, not as fun as rescuing pups living in the street, even if it can be super rewarding.

Let's say that after you look up what being a vet is truly like, you decide you still want to become a vet.

Then what do you have to do to get there?

You have to look up what kind of education you need to become a vet and what it takes to get into colleges that offer that kind of education. Then, you have to break it down. If you need a B in biology, let's say, to get accepted to that kind of degree, then you might decide that from now on, you study biology for twenty minutes three times a week. That way, you know that when you get tests, it won't be so hard. Or perhaps you just review the information you learned in class the same day so that you remember it more easily.

The BIG thing to remember with BIG goals is to first figure out if they are what you *truly* want and, secondly, break them down into SMALL pieces. You can't become a soccer pro overnight, but you can start to practice soccer for twenty minutes every day.

Setting Some Goals Right Now

> ✓ Now that you know what a goal is (something you want to achieve or create), what are some goals you'd like to have for this week?

It could be that you want to do well on a test on Monday, so you need to break that goal down. How much do you need to study every day to do well on the test? Perhaps you need to study a little extra the night before the test, too. And maybe there are some things you don't know or understand and you need to ask a teacher before the test.

It could be that you want to create a great birthday party. That's your goal. But what do you have to do to reach your goal? Come up with a good party theme? Create a list of what you need to buy? Go shopping? Make and send invites? Decorate at home? Book a place to have the party? And what are your deadlines to ensure you're ready on the day of the party?

It could be that one day you want to become a plumber and would like to find out more about plumbing to see if it's for you. Then you want to find out what you have to do—the steps you have to take—to become a plumber.

Remember that you can create small everyday goals, too! Little things you want to create. Such as having half an hour to spend with your dog at night, calling your grandma, or baking a cake.

As we discussed when talking about making a decision about what camp to attend, it's also great to set intentions for what you want out of experiences. For example, with the birthday party: What do you want out of the experience? Enjoy your time with friends? Connect with new people? Introduce friends to each other? Remember this on the day when things don't always go perfectly. Even if the cake falls over, or your favorite friend doesn't show up, you can still achieve your goals/intentions if you just stay focused.

Another example would be if you've promised to babysit your baby brother and have planned to have fun bonding with him and playing video games. Let's say the power goes out. Now you can't play video games. But you could play a board game or some other game and still bond and have fun.

With goals, instead of letting life happen to you, you decide what you want to happen and set out to achieve it.

What You've Learned in This Chapter

A goal is something you decide you want to do/achieve/create. It's different from just being a dream as you take steps to achieve it.

If you have a dream, such as becoming a professional ballerina, it's important to figure out what the life of a ballerina is truly like before you turn it into a goal and start taking steps to achieve it.

Some goals are short-term goals—something you want to achieve today or this week.

Other goals are long-term goals, like wanting to save up some money over the next year.

If you have a big goal, like wanting to save a certain amount of money by the end of the year, you break it down into smaller goals. Such as doing some chores you might get paid for every week or selling cookies to the neighbors.

Instead of "seeing what's happening" on any given day (although we all need some days like that), we can decide what we want to see happening and go out and create it. Perhaps your goal today is to do your homework so fast that you have more time to spend with your horse. And your goal when spending time with your horse is to connect and really try to understand what your horse wants and not just what you want out of your riding session.

Setting goals helps us figure out what we most want to do. It also helps us figure out a way to do it.

It's one thing to say you want to go to Paris or New York. It's another to start saving money every week so you know you CAN go to Paris or New York.

Goals help us make our dreams a reality.

And if you don't know what to do to reach your goals? Don't know the steps to take? You ask some adults. There's always someone out there who can help you make your dreams a reality.

Part 2: Social Skills

CHAPTER SIX

Becoming a Communication Superhero

Learn the basics of how to speak and write in such a way that people respond better to you. And figure out why people respond the way they do to how you move, dress, and speak!

Do you know why some people get instantly happy, scared, or sad when they see you?

That's what we're going to figure out in this chapter!

Let's start with looking at how you feel in different situations.

How do you feel when you sit next to someone who smells bad? You don't feel great, do you? Because smells affect how we feel.

How do you feel when someone smiles at you? You feel good, right? Because someone who smiles at us signals that they are happy to see us or simply that they are happy. And if they're happy, it's easier for us to have a good time with them.

If you do something good for someone and they thank you, you feel pretty good about yourself, don't you? But if they don't say anything at all, you might end up feeling disappointed or even thinking they don't care about you.

How do you think someone feels if they walk into a room hunching their shoulders and looking down on the ground?

Actually, try it out. Ask someone around you to walk in front of you. Ask them to hunch their shoulders (i.e. pull them up) and look down at the floor. Then try talking to them while they're still looking at the floor.

How do you think that person is feeling? And how is it making you feel?

Now, let them walk into the room with their back straight, smiling, and looking you in the eyes. How do you think they are feeling? And how are they making you feel?

Humans are kind of like chemicals—whenever we interact, we react.

If you pour some vinegar or lemon juice into a glass and add some baking soda, it will start to fizz.

Now, imagine your moods and your body language being different chemicals. If you smile, that's one chemical. If you cry, that's another chemical. If you keep fidgeting with your hands, that's another chemical.

The people you meet will react to those chemicals.

The Power of Body Language: Non-verbal Cues

How we use our body often communicates how we feel. People who walk with a straight back look confident. People who walk with hunched shoulders don't look confident, or simply look uncomfortable.

The things that make you look confident include:

- Looking people in the eyes (but not staring)
- Having good posture, like a straight back
- Keeping your hands and feet still (not fidgeting or clenching and unclenching your hands)
- Having a firm handshake
- Speaking in a voice that can be heard (i.e. not too quiet)

- Relaxing your face (when we get nervous, we tend to tense some muscles)
- Keeping your body language open (i.e. you don't cross your arms and legs)

Things that make you look nervous:

- Staring at the ground
- Darting your eyes about the room (i.e. looking around constantly)
- Fidgeting with your hands
- Tapping your foot on the floor
- Closing your body off—crossing your hands, arms, and legs
- Hunching over (slouching or hunching your shoulders)
- Biting your lip
- Biting your fingernails
- Speaking so quietly people can't hear you
- Avoiding eye contact
- Speaking very fast
- Speaking with a high-pitched voice

Now, the above are just some of the things that might show you how someone is feeling. You could be hugging yourself and looking down on the ground, not because you're nervous, or shy, but because you're cold! Or perhaps you had bad news and you're sad.

The important thing to remember? When we look at people, we read them kind of like the way we read a book—we decide just by looking at them if they're happy, sad, angry, nervous, and so forth.

It's good to ask yourself if you are making assumptions about how people feel or if you're truly finding out how they feel!

It's also good to check your own body language to see what signals you're sending others!

Dressing the Part

Do you judge people by how they dress?

Ever seen a skater wearing skating clothes? Immediately, you think they are a skater.

Likewise, if you see someone wearing ballet clothes, you think they are a dancer.

When we go to parties, we usually wear clothes we think look better than everyday clothes. They are special clothes. Not only do we look good in them, it shows whoever is holding the party that we respect them. We are looking nice for their sake.

That's why, if someone shows up in shabby clothes to a party, people might get offended.

Just like we read people's body language, we read them by looking at their clothes. If we like their clothes, we're more likely to think of them as someone we could be friends with.

Everyone has different styles and more or less money to spend on clothes. Just do your best to wear clothes that are right for what you are doing (such as wearing nice clothes to a party) and put in an effort to look good.

I'm not saying you should be vain where you have an overly high opinion of yourself. But when people see you the first time, they make a judgment about who you are based on how you act and what you look and smell like. So if you smell good and wear clothes you feel *show who you really are* and use body language that communicates who you are, people are more likely to see the real you.

What You Say and How You Say It Matters

Remember how I mentioned that if you do something nice for someone and they don't thank you, you might feel sad? If they thank you, on the other hand, you feel happy. You know that what you did mattered to them.

Imagine walking into a shop. The owner looks up from a magazine grumpily, frowns, then looks down again.

Now, imagine instead, that when you walk into the shop, the owner looks up from the magazine, smiles, and says, "Hello, welcome to my shop. I'm happy to see you here today. Can I help you with anything?"

Which scenario would make you feel better? You can even try acting this out with your parents or friends. One of you acts the part of the shopkeeper and the other the customer.

Just like our body language is kind of like chemicals, so are our words—people react to them.

That's why adults often say that "please" and "thank you" will get you far in life. Because people respond to what you say to them. If you use polite words, people are a lot more willing to help you out. Chances are, they will also like you better.

But here's the trick: you can't do just the words without your body language. If you walk into a shop and mumble quietly while looking down at the floor, even if you say nice things, the shop owner probably won't feel that you like them. Instead, they might feel like you're scared of them.

You have to match your words with your actions. If you've just met someone and you shake their hand firmly, look them in the eye, and say, "Nice to meet you," they will believe you mean it.

If you, instead, look down at the ground, give a weak handshake, and mumble, "Nice to meet you," chances are they won't think you mean it.

Go ahead. Try it out with someone. Walk up and shake their hand, using different body language.

Now, imagine your parents telling you to go to bed early. But you don't want to. So you stomp your foot and say something nasty. Will they let you stay up longer? No.

If, on the other hand, you said, "Please can I have five minutes more if I get ready for bed at super speed? I would really, really appreciate it," they might just give you an extra five minutes.

Politeness gets you far. That especially holds true for when you get irritated or angry.

Does one of your siblings perhaps like to play loud music you don't like?

When they do it, maybe you feel like screaming, "Turn off that stupid music, it's driving me nuts. I'm trying to chat with my friend."

Chances are, they will get angry if you're getting angry with them.

If, on the other hand, you say, "Please can you be super sweet and turn down the music a bit? I know you love it, I'm just trying to speak with a friend of mine. Please?" they might turn down the music.

> Do you notice how you get sad if people yell at you or get upset with you? Or perhaps you get angry?
>
> One or the other, right?
>
> So if you want someone to do something for you, do you think the best way is to get angry or be polite?

You can still be FIRM even if you're polite. Your baby sister cannot cover your bed with her dolls. But if you ask her kindly not to do it, and hug her while you do it, she's much more likely to do as you ask.

Ask and Receive: The Importance of Clear Communication

The easiest way to get what you want?

Ask for it.

People often think other people are mind readers.

Really?

Really.

Have you ever felt sad and just wished someone would see it and help you feel better?

Or maybe your brother playing with a certain toy that makes a lot of noise irritates you ALL day. You show your irritation by frowning, pulling faces, sighing, and so forth. Then when he picks up the toy again at night, you snap and start shouting at him to stop playing with it. He gets upset because you're shouting at him; you're upset because you feel he's been ignoring you all day. But you never told him outright to stop playing with the toy. You simply assumed he would know you were irritated.

Or perhaps you've hinted to your parents all year long that you want a bike. Come your birthday, you get a pair of rollerblades. Perhaps you've mentioned rollerblades as being fun, too. As you didn't say specifically that you wanted a bike for your birthday, they went with the rollerblades.

If you want something, deliver the message loud and clear and be polite about it.

The Silent Movie Exercise

Did you know that when movies first came out, they were silent? Yet people watched them and felt they understood how the actors in the movies felt.

Try this.

Turn off the sound of a movie and watch for five minutes. With the sound off, guess how the characters are feeling just by looking at their faces.

In everyday life, we don't often think about how we know if someone is upset, happy, sad, excited, and so forth. But we can learn to pay attention and see when we are making assumptions about how someone is feeling based on their body language and how others might make assumptions about us because of our own body language.

With a friend or parent, pretend you're in a silent movie. You can act out different situations where you practice being confident. Perhaps you pretend to walk into a store and confidently ask the shop manager to buy some clothes. You can also pretend to be at a job interview, a party, or with friends. Pay attention to how you act and the expressions on your face.

Here's a tip: When we act happy and confident, we often start to feel happy and confident.

What You've Learned in This Chapter

How we smell.

How we move our body.

How we talk.

What words we use.

What clothes we wear.

Those are all things that other people look at when "reading" us. They use them as clues to figure out what we are thinking and feeling. And how they react to us depends on all of the above.

By acting out different situations, you can learn to use body language that helps others get a better impression of you. You can practice doing things that make you look confident. Doing those things often also makes you feel confident!

Using your words correctly is also important. Be polite. Whatever you say, say it nicely.

When speaking or writing, you also have to be clear. Say what you want. Hinting only causes confusion, and chances are you won't get what you want if you only hint at it!

CHAPTER SEVEN

Spreading Kindness

If you've ever felt warmth spread in your heart after someone was kind to you, you know the importance of kindness. We will look more at how important it truly is and why you should be kind when other people are rude.

Words and actions are kind of like magic.

Why?

Because they have the power to make other people (and animals) feel and believe things about themselves and the world.

If you treat someone nicely, they feel good and chances are they'll think that you like them and that they are a good person.

If you treat someone badly, they feel bad and might think they aren't good enough to be liked.

If you tell someone they are great, they might believe you. If they do, they will act great because they *think* they are great.

If you tell someone they are bad, they might believe you. If they do, they will act badly because they *think* they are bad.

Emma walked up to Karl in school. "Hey, Karl, I just want to say that I love the picture you're painting."

Karl was really shy, but when Emma complimented him, his face lit up. "Thanks, Emma."

Karl wasn't sure if his painting was good enough, but because Emma liked it, he decided to enter a competition.

Karl won the competition and shyly went up to Emma in class. "Thank you, Emma, for saying you liked my painting the other week. I entered it into a competition and won. I wouldn't have done it if it wasn't for you."

Emma was happy that her words had made a difference, and the two became friends.

Why Are People Mean?

People are different.

Some people are born with conditions that make their brains different. That means that sometimes they get angry or sad more easily. They find it hard to control their emotions.

However, most people who are rude to others are rude because they have been hurt at some point. They feel pain inside and that makes them act badly. Or they grew up in a place where they had to defend themselves all the time and became aggressive just to cope. That probably also makes them hurt inside.

Have you ever felt sad or upset? How did you act then? Were you nice to everyone around you? Or did you, perhaps, get angry?

Often when we're upset, we act out. And some kids have a difficult time at home or at school and act out a lot. They need to learn to stop acting that way. We are all responsible for what we do. But what should you do if someone is mean to you? Or teases you? Should you try to hurt them back?

No. Because then they hurt you again. Then you hurt them. And so on. It never stops. It becomes what people like to call a vicious cycle.

That's how you start a war.

If someone is nasty to you, tell them to stop. They have no right to treat you that way. No one does. Don't be mean in return; simply tell them to stop and take it to an adult if they don't stop after you ask them to.

A good thing to remember is that if we think someone is nasty, we don't want to be like them.

If someone says something to you that you think is rude, disrespectful, hurtful, or mean, you shouldn't respond in the same way. Why? Because then you become like them. You become someone who isn't being nice. And how will that make you feel about being you?

I want to feel good about myself, so I act nicely towards others.

> If you close your eyes for a moment and imagine being nice to someone, how does it feel? Does it feel good or bad?
>
> Now, close your eyes and imagine being mean to someone. How does that feel? Does it make you feel good or bad?

Even when other people are bad, we can choose to be good.

Consider standing up to bullies the way ninjas do—when someone attacks, they stop the fight. They aren't trying to hurt their opponent, simply disarming them and ensuring they aren't fighting anymore.

Remembering Who You Are—A Superstar

If someone tells you something mean, you have to remember that it isn't true.

Let's say you have purple hair. So when someone walks up to you and says "Your pink hair is so ugly," do you feel bad? No. Because your hair isn't pink. It's purple. Clearly the person isn't seeing right.

It's the same when someone tells you something nasty. You don't have to feel bad about it, because *it isn't true*.

Confident people are people who know their own worth. That means they know they are good. So when other people tell them they are not, they just shrug their shoulders.

Even if you do something wrong, or make a mistake, you don't have to feel bad if someone tells you off for it. So what if you aren't great at swimming? Or you just did something stupid. Everyone does from time to time.

YOU are still great.

Exercise

Draw a picture of yourself and write down who you are. Get an adult to help you list all the good things about being you.

Perhaps you are kind. Great at skiing. Helpful with your brother. Nice to animals. Good at writing. Love swimming.

Whatever it is, write it all down. These aren't necessarily super skills, it's just who you are.

Next time someone is being mean to you, ask yourself if what they said is true. If not, why feel bad about it? You are a great person and should hang out with people who treat you like that.

Walking in Someone Else's Shoes

Having empathy means putting yourself in someone else's shoes and imagining why they act the way they do.

As a child, it's easy to laugh at other kids who are "strange." They wear weird clothes. They smell funny. They speak funny. But have you ever asked *why* they do that? And seen the person *underneath*?

Just because someone has a parent who can't afford nice clothes (or doesn't understand style), doesn't mean they aren't a cool person.

If someone is shy, perhaps it's because someone was, or is, very mean to them at home. Or perhaps it's because one of their parents died and they are sad. If you get to know them, you might discover that they are really kind and funny.

If someone is talking all the time, which is really irritating, perhaps it is because s/he is nervous. And when they relax, they're a fun person to be around.

The day something happens to you that upsets you and makes you act funny, you probably wish that someone will be there to ask you what's wrong, instead of judging you for what you're doing.

Even if you don't want to make friends with someone, you can still be nice to them.

Remember what I said in the beginning of this chapter? Your words are kind of like magic. You have the power to make people feel good. So use it!

> Elsie went to visit her grandma in the woods. They were having tea and cake in the kitchen when they heard something howling.
>
> "What's that?" Elsie asked.

"Sounds like a dog," Grandma said. "Let us have a look."

Sure enough, they found an injured dog not far from Grandma's house.

"Oh no, he looks really skinny and sick," Elsie said.

Grandma looked angry. "He looks like he's been mistreated by humans and then let out into the forest when they got tired of him. We should help him." But as they walked closer, the dog started snapping at them.

"Uh oh, he's angry," Elsie said. "You used to be a vet, what should we do?"

"We need to give him food with a sedative to get him to calm down. Then I can take him home and clean him up. He won't survive out here on his own. Now, I want you to run home and fetch my vet bag and some of the steak in the fridge, and I'll wait here for you."

Elsie ran back to Grandma's house as fast as her legs could carry her, got everything she needed, and returned to Gran, who was still talking calmly to the dog.

"He's stopped howling!" Elsie noted.

"Yes, I kept talking to him in a calm manner," Gran said. Then she prepared the meat with the sedative for the dog. "Let's feed him this. It's a special sedative that works for dogs. Never try this on your own unless you've been trained as the wrong dosage can harm the dog and you should never approach an angry dog by yourself as it could have a disease, maybe even rabies, which can potentially kill you if you get bitten and don't get medical treatment," she cautioned.

"I promise."

Gran threw the dog the meat, and being hungry, he ate it up and was soon snoozing.

"Thank goodness," Gran said, putting on a pair of protective gloves from her bag and going to pick up the dog.

"Why wouldn't he let us come close earlier?" Elsie asked.

"He was frightened."

"But why? We didn't do anything to him," Elsie protested as they walked towards Gran's house, Gran carrying the dog and Elsie Gran's vet bag.

"Other people must have been treating him badly. That's why he's in such bad condition."

"But we're not them," Elsie said, looking offended. "I'd never hurt a dog."

Gran smiled as Elsie opened the door to her house. "I know you wouldn't. But this dog doesn't. And remember that when you deal with humans too—if they are often angry and bark loudly, chances are someone else hurt them."

They took the dog inside and Gran cleaned him up and stitched up a bad wound he had while he was still sleeping. When he awoke, he was one clean puppy! He was also fed lots of food and medicine. And after a while of being looked after and eating well, he started being less aggressive. He got used to Gran and Elsie, who would visit him every day after school.

After a few months, the pup, now named Mr. Simpson, was much happier and never even barked at Elsie or Gran, but whenever he met new people, he started growling.

"Don't do that, sit," Gran would tell him whenever he barked or growled at strangers. She was always firm with him but also praised him when he did the right thing.

It took a whole year before Mr. Simpson could walk without a leash. By that time, he'd learned that most humans were nice and wouldn't get angry at them for no reason.

From then on, whenever Elsie met people who were mean to her for no reason, she felt sorry for them. She told them firmly she wouldn't accept them being mean, but she also tried showing them kindness. She suspected someone else had been mean to them in the past.

What You've Learned in This Chapter

Your words are like magic—you have the power to make people feel good and bad.

Some people are different from us and we might not want to be friends with them, but we can still be nice to them. We can still help them feel good.

If someone is mean to you and you're mean to them back, what do you think will happen?

They will be mean to you again, right? And then you will be mean.

What's more, you probably won't like yourself very much because you aren't acting nicely.

You can choose to be nice when others are mean.

You still have to tell them to stop being mean and put an end to it, but you don't have to sink to their level. You don't have to become mean, too.

It's important to remember that people who are mean usually feel hurt or are trying to defend themselves as they are used to other people being mean to them. That doesn't make what they are doing right, but it helps you understand why they are doing it.

Some people also have mental conditions that make it harder for them to control their emotions. That might mean they get sad or angry more easily, or get super happy, then super upset. This might hold true for some (but certainly not all) people with autism, sensory processing disorders, or ADHD. People who are bi-polar also suffer from mood swings. Think about when you're really tired or hungry—that can make you grumpy, angry, and sad more easily. Some people have brain imbalances that make them feel like that all the time.

Or they simply can't control their impulses, so when they're happy, they might hug you without thinking if you like it or not, or if they get angry, they might lash out and say or do something nasty. That's why they get therapy and/or medication to help their brains become more balanced and help them control their emotions and impulses.

If you feel it's difficult to control your emotions or impulses, you might want to try meditation and breathing exercises. Those have been shown to help us feel better and stay calmer. There are many apps for this, and you can also ask an adult for help.

If meditation and breathing exercises don't help, you might want to talk to your parents about seeing a therapist who can teach you more about how the brain works and what you can do to be happy and in control.

Remember who you are. You are a great person. So if someone says something mean to you, you know it isn't true. You don't have to feel bad about it.

Part 3: Practical Skills

CHAPTER EIGHT

Dealing with Emergencies

Basic knowledge on what to do in an emergency

Help! There's an emergency.

What do you do?

That depends on the emergency. So let's have a look at the different types of emergencies that can happen.

(And don't worry—most never happen. But if they do, you will know what to do!)

Emergency Basics: Be Prepared and Stay Calm

Emergencies do happen. It can be something small, like someone scraping their knee pretty badly and needing stitches.

It can be something big, like someone having a heart attack.

The good thing is, if you're prepared and know what to do, you might be able to help. And that, in turn, can help the person who is injured.

The number one rule in an emergency? Stay calm and call for help.

How do you stay calm?

People who study the brain say that those who meditate and do mindfulness exercises tend to stay calm even when difficult things happen. We will learn more about that in another chapter.

Calling for help means calling your local emergency number (such as 911 in most of America and 112 in most of Europe) and alerting an adult near you (if there is anyone) of what's happening.

Dealing with Emergencies

Here are some things you can do to be prepared for an emergency:

- Attend a first aid class for children—the Scouts, 4H, and other community groups might organize one, but if you're not part of an organization like that, ask if your school nurse can hold one (you can also look for online courses—ask your parents about it)

- Always have a first aid kit in your home, car, and possibly, even in your backpack—and know where exactly it is and how to use it

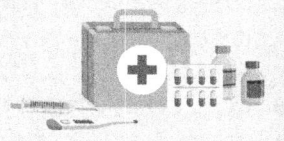

- When you travel, always carry a first aid kit and some snacks (that aren't in your actual snack/lunch bag) and a bottle of water (that you aren't planning to drink)—if you get stuck somewhere, you have something to carry you through

- If you travel somewhere cold or if you leave the city, carry extra clothing and blankets

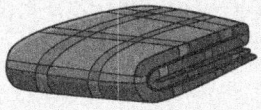

- Put emergency numbers on your phone (in some areas, you need special numbers, like where I live, we have a specific number for snake bites)

- Always keep your phone charged

- If you live in an area prone to earthquakes and other natural disasters, like hurricanes, know what to do in case it happens and, again, have an emergency kit packed

Real-Life Scenarios: Falls, Fires, and More

Let's say someone has fallen. If they hit their head or neck, don't try to move them. Just calmly chat with them and call 911 or 112 or your local emergency number. Also, call for an adult.

If someone is bleeding, what do you do? If it's a big cut of some sort, the most important thing is to stop the blood flow and call for help. You want to call for help as soon as possible!

Wounds and Injuries

If someone is bleeding, wrap something super tight around the wound, or press something against the wound (if, say, it's on the shoulder and you can't wrap it). Don't remove the pressure, or the bandage to check if the bleeding has stopped—wait for help to arrive.

Note that if there is something still stuck in the wound, like a big shard of glass, or a knife, removing it might make the bleeding worse. Wait for help. However, you also can't press *on* the shard of glass or the knife. Then you have to apply pressure *around* it. Tell emergency services over the phone what the wound looks like and ask what to do.

If someone is bleeding from the hand, or arm, you can hold the hand above their head after, or even while, you wrap it. As the heart has to pump blood around the body, it's harder for it to pump it all the way up. This helps slow the bleeding.

If someone has injured their leg, or foot, and is bleeding a lot, you can lie them down and put their leg on a pillow or rest it against something else that raises it up. That way, the leg or foot is higher up than the heart.

If someone has a small cut, or abrasion, you can simply wash it in water to get any dirt out. Then, sterilize it with some rubbing alcohol, iodine, dettol, or hydrogen peroxide (hydrogen peroxide is sometimes diluted in the bottle you buy it in, but if it's pure or has a high percentage of hydrogen peroxide, you have to dilute it first). After that, put on a plaster or bandage.

Stroke

Sometimes people have something called a stroke. It's a blood clot in their brain. A stroke can make people look and act funny, slur their words, lose control over a certain part of their body, fall to the ground, or pass out. If someone acts weird, or you see one side of their face drooping, immediately call for help using your phone and alert an adult to it, as well.

Heart Attack

Heart attacks are another thing that can make people suddenly fall down, get chest pains, or get a tingling sensation on one side of their body (usually the left side). If this happens, again, call the emergency services immediately and alert an adult if someone is nearby.

It's important to remember that you can also faint even if you aren't sick. Maybe someone with low blood pressure or who is dehydrated because they haven't had enough water stands up too quickly and faints. A person collapsing isn't always serious, nor is it always a stroke or heart attack if someone feels one side of their body go funny, but you should always call for help as you don't know.

Epileptic Attack

If someone starts shaking violently, they might have something called an epileptic attack. It's important you call the emergency services and alert an adult. If you can get them to lie down on a bed or the floor, it is also helpful as they might hurt themselves if they fall.

The most important thing to remember? If it's a big wound, you're not sure what's happening, or it seems serious, call for help. Pick up your phone and dial for emergency services and alert an adult if someone is nearby.

Remember the old saying "better safe than sorry"? It's always best to ask for help if someone is injured if you think it might be serious.

The House Is On Fire

We often joke about saying, "the house is on fire," meaning there's an emergency of some kind. Unfortunately, sometimes the house *is* on fire. What do you do?

First, let's look at what you can do to prevent a fire and have tools ready if there is a fire. Tip: you can go through this list with your parent or an adult to check if you have these things in your home.

- Install smoke alarms in every room of your home
- Check the smoke alarms once a month (and give the dog a fright! Sorry, doggie!)
- Put fire extinguishers in at least two places in the house (and choose ones that can be used on electrical and oil fires)
- Learn how to use a fire extinguisher
- Put a fire blanket in your kitchen
- Learn how to exit the house in different rooms in case of a fire
- Learn a system for remembering to turn off appliances and blow out candles (such as setting a timer when you cook something, or when you light a candle)
- Never leave anything burnable near a heat source (don't put curtains just by the stove, don't leave a candle near anything that can burn, don't hang laundry over old radiators, and so forth)
- Make sure there are keys near each exit, so it's easy to exit (you don't have to run to the kitchen to get the keys to get out)

- Install an alarm or emergency button you can press for alarm services

How to Extinguish a Fire

A fire can be extinguished in different ways.

1) You can remove the oxygen. A fire needs oxygen to survive, just like humans!
2) You can cool it down.
3) You can remove burnable materials. If there's nothing that can burn, the fire will die out. For example, a fireplace is safe because it's made of rock or metal that doesn't burn, even if the logs or gas inside the fire burn.

Here are a few popular methods for extinguishing a fire:

1) Fire extinguishers—there are different types for different types of fires
2) Water—if it's not an oil, chemical, or electrical fire, you can use water to extinguish it
3) Smothering the fire with a blanket and stomping on it and then pouring water on top
4) If it's a small electrical fire, you can throw baking soda on it to smother it
5) Large amounts of sand can smother a fire

If a fire is due to a heat source, such as the stove, turn it off. If it's an electrical device, unplug it, but use thick *dry* gloves made from plastic or leather, or wrap your hand in a thick *dry* towel so you don't get hurt.

Dennis walked into the kitchen to see that his brother, who was making french fries, had set the pot on fire.

"Step back, Pat," Dennis shouted.

Dennis picked up the lid for the pot, put it on, and turned off the stove.

Within minutes, the fire was gone.

"How did the fire die?" Pat asked.

"I removed the air," Dennis replied. "Fire needs air, or it dies. I put the lid on the pot, so when there was no more air for the fire, it died. I could have thrown a lot of sand on it, or covered it with a special fire blanket, instead. Now, I'm going to call Mom and tell her what happened."

When to Leave the House

As a general rule, if you are alone and it's not just a pot on fire, or something else that's small and can be easily extinguished, LEAVE THE HOUSE. After you've left the house call 911 and run to the nearest adult to alert them of what's happening.

If you are in the house and it's a BIG fire, *immediately* look for the best way to exit.

If there's a clear way out—run.

What to check before running:

1) Do I have a key to get out (if one is needed)?
2) Do I have something to smash a window with if I can't open one?

If you have to walk through the house and the fire is widespread, pull your shirt over your nose and mouth. Pick up a fire extinguisher if one is standing next to you and run towards where you think you can most easily get out while dodging the fire. Before opening the door, wrap your hand with your shirt or some cloth in case the handle is hot.

Dealing with Emergencies

If you cannot open the door, try to open a window, or smash it with the fire extinguisher.

DO NOT OPEN A WINDOW TO GET FRESH AIR WHILE WAITING TO GET RESCUED. The oxygen will only make the fire worse.

If you are on fire, what should you do? Pick the answer you think is best.

- A) Run to the shower or bath and turn it on
- B) Find a fire extinguisher and spray yourself
- C) Stop, drop, and roll, protecting your face, while calling for help

A shower might sound like the perfect idea, but unless you're in the bathroom already, stop, drop, and roll is the best. Be sure to cover your face while you roll. By rolling on the fire, you smother it (remove the oxygen).

If you see someone else catch fire, immediately tell them to stop, drop, and roll while protecting their face. Find a large blanket or duvet to wrap them in to extinguish the flames faster, or use a nearby fire extinguisher to spray them while they're rolling on the floor. If you get a blanket, pour water on top once you've rolled them in it.

What You've Learned in This Chapter

If there's an emergency, stay calm and call for help.

Dial the number to the local emergency services AND alert an adult.

If someone has a small wound, you can clean it up, sterilize it, and put on a bandage.

If someone is bleeding a lot, try to stop the blood flow by pressing against the wound (but not against something like a big shard of glass sticking out of it, then you have to apply pressure *around* it—don't remove it) and calling for help. If you can, keep the wound above their head.

If someone has fallen, don't try to move them if they have hit or injured their back, neck, or head. Just call for help immediately.

Do what you can to prevent fires. If you are on fire, remember to stop, drop, and roll while protecting your face. If someone else is on fire, you can also get a blanket to roll them in and spray water on top. But FIRST, have them stop, drop, and roll.

If there's a fire in your home that's not contained (i.e. it's spreading to more than a pot or similar), leave the house through the nearest exit and call for help.

If it's a contained fire (it's very small), you use the nearest fire extinguisher to extinguish it. Always make sure to have one in each room and one smoke alarm in each room.

If the house is on fire, don't open a window for fresh air—the oxygen will help the fire spread. Only open a window or door to get out. If you can, wrap something over your mouth and nose, such as pulling up the shirt you're wearing if you have to run through a fire. If you have to go through flames, douse yourself in water first if you can.

Remember that metal gets hot in a fire, so if you have to touch a door handle, first wrap your hand.

Fire can be extinguished by removing the oxygen, removing burnable materials, or cooling the fire down. Water can be used *unless* it's an electrical, oil, or chemical fire.

Set up a fire escape route in every room and make sure there are keys to open windows or doors by those exits.

CHAPTER NINE

Becoming a Chore Master

How to get stuff done and have fun while doing it

Chores. Ugh.

Yeah, we all feel that way.

The thing about life? We have chores.

Everything worth doing in life, from taking care of a dog to looking after a home comes with chores. Even you come with chores attached—you need to look after yourself.

The good thing? There are ways to do your chores *faster* and have more *fun* when doing them.

Mastering Your Chores

Here are some tips for making chores more fun:

- Set a timer and see how fast you can do them

- Play music while doing them

- Listen to an audiobook while doing them

- Give yourself a reward (or ask your parents for one) if you do them really fast *and* really well

Remember the chapter about goals? How you can break things down into smaller things to make them easier to conquer? Like you can't do EVERYTHING to prepare for your birthday party today, but you can do one thing a day and in ten days have the most epic party ever.

Chores are the same. If the thought of spending *an hour* cleaning your room makes you want to hide under your bed, break it down to just ten minutes cleaning every day or focus on just one or two areas. You'll probably end up with the cleanest room you've ever had, and it won't even feel difficult!

Look at the chores you have to do throughout the week. Then get an adult to help you with how much time you need to spend on them every day to make it easy.

Another tip? Do what you like the least first.

Yep. By doing it first, it's out of the way. Everything after that will feel like a breeze.

Check the Facts Before You Begin

If there are chores that involve appliances, detergents, and other things that might, if used wrongly, damage things or hurt you, it's important you learn the facts before you use them.

Always ask your parents or other adults about detergents and appliances before you use them, and if you're unsure of something, look it up online, or ask a specialist, if you can. If it's an appliance, you can also read the instruction manual. Remember that when you look things up online, you should check more than one site to verify the facts. Not everything written online is true.

Any chore you have is worth looking up online if you want to find out ways to do it better, or faster! There are a ton of "hacks" for most things.

If you are doing chores around the house, always check with your parents or guardian what exactly they want you to do.

If you have to clean the house, chances are your parents have special detergents for special things. Like one cleaning detergent for the bathroom and another for the kitchen.

And here's the deal—if you use the wrong detergent on something, it might get ruined. For example, if you use a detergent with bleach on a painted table, you might bleach the table!

So ask an adult to tell you *exactly* what to do before you begin. They might not even think about you needing instructions because they're so used to doing something one way that they think you already know!

Safe and Sound: Using Appliances with Care

If you have a chore that involves using appliances, such as the laundry machine, stove, or vacuum cleaner, get an adult to explain it to you and show you the first time you use it. (And the second and third time, too, if you can't remember what they said the first time! Better safe than sorry.)

A lot of machines are tricky, need cleaning after use, and can be dangerous if used wrongly. For example, you can't use a regular vacuum cleaner to get rid of water on the floor. That can lead to you getting electrocuted (with special vacuum machines, on the other hand, it's safe)! And if you stick your fingers in the garbage disposal and start it, your fingers can get cut off. So always check with an adult before you use any kind of appliance!

The Cleaning Game: Making Cleaning and Tidying Up Fun!

Below are some tips for winning at the cleaning and tidying game!

Laundry

If you are doing the laundry, sort it into dark and light colors.

Always check the label of the piece of clothing to find out if it can be machine washed (some things should only be dry-cleaned) and what temperature it should be washed in. If you wash certain fabrics in too hot water, they might shrink.

Also check if something can be tumble-dried or should be hung up to dry.

As each washing machine is different, you need to talk to an adult to understand how your machine works and how much laundry detergent is needed. There are different cycles for different kinds of washing, too.

Some clothing needs ironing. Now, that's a science unto itself! If the iron is too hot, some fabrics will melt, but if it's not hot enough, you won't get the wrinkles out. There are ironing instructions on clothes, but the first couple of times, ask an adult how to read the labels and show you how to work with the iron. Then, you can do it yourself after you learn how to. And while some irons turn off automatically, not all do, so be sure it is off and unplugged after using.

Once the laundry is done, you need to fold it. The best way to learn? Either ask your parents or watch videos on YouTube. You wouldn't believe it, but there are ninja folding people out there! You can actually have a lot of fun folding your clothes . . . and time yourself to see how fast you can do it.

After that, it's time to put the clothes away. By putting them away nicely, they don't get wrinkled. You also know where to find them when you get dressed! Otherwise, how much time would you spend looking for clothes to wear every day?

Washing Dishes

Washing dishes by hand is pretty easy. You can fill your sink with hot water (but make sure it is not scalding) and dishwashing liquid, soak the dishes in it, then scrub them with a sponge, rinse them, and dry them. You might also want to wear gloves to protect your hands from the detergent and the heat of the water.

When doing the dishes, it's important to check that you actually removed all the food and fat from an item. If an item still feels fatty, oily, or slippery after rinsing it, add some extra dishwashing liquid on the sponge, swipe it on the item before rinsing with water.

Cleaning the Floors

Cleaning the floors usually requires that you use a vacuum cleaner and then a mop to make sure they're squeaky clean. But you can't mop a carpet. Likewise, sometimes your parents want you to use different detergents for different rooms when mopping. Some detergents can, for example, destroy wooden flooring. So check with your parents before scrubbing the floors!

As for the vacuum cleaner, only use it on dry surfaces unless it has a special setting for wet floors. Usually there's a button you can press depending on whether you're vacuuming a carpet or the floor. Check with your parents how to use it! And make sure to empty it regularly.

Dusting

You can dust using a cloth and a little bit of water. That will remove dust off most surfaces. The feather dusters look much cooler, but all they do is stir dust into the air. If your parents have wood or fabric furniture that can't handle water, use a microfiber cloth to wipe instead.

Other Chores

These are just a few ideas for how to do different chores. You might have to take out the garbage or make beds.

The most important part? Check with your parents how to do something before you begin. Everyone has a different idea of how it should be done!

What You've Learned in This Chapter

Make chores fun and complete them faster by setting a timer or timing yourself. Reward yourself when you get everything done on time! You can also listen to audiobooks or music while performing chores.

If you have a lot of chores, or one chore that's really boring, break it down so you only do a little bit every day.

Always ask your parents how to do something new before you start. Chances are, they will want it done a certain way. There might also be special cleaning detergents you should or should not use or machinery that can be dangerous if you don't know how to use it. Before using appliances, always read the instructions and get an adult to guide you through it.

CHAPTER TEN

Becoming a Super Foodie

Knowing the difference between food and food

Food is good for you. You need lots to grow strong. But you need the *right* kinds of foods.

What do I mean by that?

I mean some foods are good for the body—like vegetables and some meats and grains.

Other foods, like candy, aren't great for the body. They are *treats*. They are good for celebrating things and enjoying ourselves, but we shouldn't eat too much of them.

The Foods That Make Your Body Happy

You might know this from biology class, but the different nutrients found in food go on to build our body. They are kind of like the bricks that make up the house (our body) that hosts us!

For example, you need protein (found in large amounts in beans, leafy greens, meat, nuts, eggs, and dairy) to build muscles.

Some foods, like fruits and vegetables, contain a lot of nutrients, such as vitamins and minerals. They also contain something called antioxidants. Think of antioxidants as little superheroes fighting off the bad guys. This is why you often hear adults telling you to eat your fruit and veg!

Other foods, like refined carbohydrates or carbs (white flour, white rice, sugar, and so forth) contain a lot of energy but little nutrients. We need energy, but it's better to get it from foods that haven't been refined, like brown rice and flour, as they also contain more nutrients. Plus, whole grains take longer for the body to break down, meaning you get energy over a longer period of time, instead of a spike of energy and then . . . nothing.

The number one rule for choosing great ingredients?

Choose whole foods.

What? The whole apple instead of a piece of apple?

Nope. Just ingredients that haven't been refined or processed. Brown rice is a whole food. White rice is not. Steak is a whole food. Sausages are not.

If you go into a shop and buy fruits, vegetables, whole grain flours, nuts, beans, pieces of meat, milk, and so forth, you're buying whole foods.

You can buy some processed foods, like marmalade, or chocolate, but you should buy *less* of them and *more* of the whole foods.

Think of them like treats.

You also want to balance your meals so you get all the bricks for your house (i.e. all the nutrition you need). You need protein, fat, carbs, vitamins, and minerals. Buy lots of veggies (in all colors of the rainbow—try to vary what you eat) and some whole grains, nuts, beans and pulses, fruit, berries, dairy, eggs, meat, and fish.

By choosing a little bit of everything, you end up with something known as a varied diet.

Read the Label

"Dude, what's in that thing? It looks deadly."

"I don't know. It tastes good."

"Didn't you read the label?"

"Nah, Dan said it tasted good."

> The boy picks up the candy wrapper. "It says here it contains some weird coloring, hydrogenated vegetable oils, high-glucose corn syrup, and preservatives. And not the natural kind of preservatives and colorants. It might look and taste good, but it's not good *for you.*"

Something that's really important when shopping for food is reading the label.

What does it contain? Some ingredients are whole foods—like wholemeal flour. Others are refined foods, like corn syrup. For example, you can buy candy sweetened by real fruit juice (even if it's a concentrate so it's been refined) and colored by blueberry powder, or you can buy candy made with high-fructose corn syrup colored by man-made colorants.

Both versions contain sugar, but high-fructose corn syrup is considered worse as it's super refined. So it's broken down by the body super fast and gives you a massive sugar rush . . . and after that you might not feel so great.

Eating too much sugar, especially refined sugar, can lead to a disease called diabetes (talk to your parents about this or research on it online).

There are also things like colorants and preservatives that may or may not be good for you. Some additives, like colorants and preservatives are natural, others are not. And some are better for the body than others.

For example, blueberry powder is a colorant, but it's not bad for you—it's just blueberry. And blueberries are very good for your body. But some man-made colorants might not be so good for you. That means that while you can use food colorants for birthday cakes, you don't want to be eating them every day!

Another thing to look at on the label is the expiry date. If something has gone off, it can make you sick if you eat it. So buying yogurt that goes off tomorrow isn't a great idea if you plan to eat it two or three days from now.

If something doesn't have an expiry label, such as a piece of fruit, you can usually look and smell to see if it's still fresh.

Kitchen Tools 101

Kitchens can be fun . . . and confusing. There are different types of knives, graters, blenders, and so forth.

To help you learn how to use them, chat with an adult before you decide to cook something. For example, you might want to make a toasted sandwich. Which knife do you use to cut the bread? How do you use the grater to grate the cheese?

Instead of trying to learn everything at once, it's good to do it this way: find a recipe, and before you start cooking, ask an adult to help you understand the tools you'll need to cook it.

Blenders, stoves, microwaves, and knives can be dangerous if you use them the wrong way. That's why it's so important to speak with an adult first.

For example, if you put the wrong thing in a microwave, it can explode!

And if you forget the oven on, it can cause a fire (always set a timer when you cook so you are reminded to check the food!).

> If you leave the lid off a blender and start it, you'll have food splattered all over the kitchen. And if you leave a fork or some other utensil in the blender and start it, both the utensil and the blender might break! Worse yet, if you stick your fingers in a blender, you can cut yourself on the blades.

Learning to Make the Recipes You Love—Family Cooking Fun

Something really fun when you get started with cooking is asking your parents, or grandparents, about the recipes they love to cook (and that you love to eat!). Almost every family has some "secret family recipes." Even if you don't live with your "real" parents, it can help you to bond with the people looking after you.

That won't just make you a great cook, it will make your relatives happy that you want to learn some dishes from them! And it's usually easier to learn from a real person than watching a video online or reading a recipe in a book, but that can be lots of fun, too!

You can also ask your relatives to write the recipes down and stick them all in a special family recipe book. It can be a scrapbook (so you get to see all your relatives' handwritten notes), or you can even create a book online and print it!

Don't have a lot of relatives? Ask your friends and their families for their secret family recipes.

Easy Treats—Cooking Made Simple

When we talk about healthy foods and eating well, it's easy to think your life is over (sort of). If you have to give up eating all the "fun" stuff, what's the point?

But there are plenty of treats you can make yourself that are super simple and super yummy!

For example, make a smoothie or juice, then freeze it as popsicles/ice lollies! You can either freeze the juice or smoothie in small containers (like small yogurt containers) that you stick a spoon in, or you can buy molds especially for the purpose. Sometimes they even have these molds in local supermarkets, but otherwise, your parents can help you find where they are sold online. For example, online markets will be sure to stock them.

It's the perfect treat for a hot day!

Also, on a hot day, frozen grapes are delicious. Personally, I like frozen blueberries and frozen mango, too. You can also make super delicious mango smoothies—just blend together frozen mango and raspberries with a little bit of honey and vegan milk. If you want to make it healthy, add in a handful of raw spinach or curly kale—you won't taste it, but you'll get your greens! Just don't add more than a handful because then you *will* taste it!

A quick way of making ice cream? Peel, chop, and freeze bananas so you always have a nice supply in the freezer. On a hot day, take some out and blend them in a blender. This leaves you with something resembling soft-serve ice cream! You can add a bit of cacao and honey if you want chocolate ice cream, or vanilla if you want vanilla ice cream.

If you don't like bananas, you can use coconut cream instead, but you'll need more honey to make it sweet.

Fruity soft serves can also be made if you blend ripe avocado flesh (the avo should be soft-ish to the touch) that's NOT frozen, with frozen berries, honey, and a splash of water or vegan milk. You need a a high-quality blender for this, however, as it doesn't become smooth otherwise.

If you have a good blender, another quick and healthy fix is chocolate mousse. Simply blend ripe avocado flesh with cacao, honey, and vegan milk, or coconut cream.

Don't believe me when I say avo can make for a great dessert? Try it out!

Another treat to try is frozen bananas. Put a peeled banana on a stick, roll it in some melted chocolate, then roll it in chopped nuts. Freeze on a tray or in a container.

Love chocolate and nuts? Mix together your favorite nut butter with cacao and honey. Form little balls and enjoy as "truffles."

You can also make chocolate balls by combining melted coconut butter with honey, cacao, and oats. Once done, you can roll them in desiccated coconut, if you like. Or just put them in the refrigerator. They'll be ready to eat in an hour or two.

Want to bake a treat? This is one of the simplest ones to try!

Buy some frozen puff pastry from your local store. (Remember to check the ingredients! You don't want a dough with strange preservatives or hydrogenated vegetable oils!)

Defrost the puff pastry.

Preheat the oven to 350–400F or about 175–185 degrees Celsius.

Line a baking tray with baking paper.

Roll out the puff pastry and place it atop the baking paper.

Cut out the core and slice the apples and pears in thin slices (I like to use more apples than pears, but to each their own). Put in a bowl and sprinkle with lemon juice (1–2 tbsp), cinnamon, ginger, and brown sugar OR honey (1–3 tbsp). Sprinkle with a generous dusting of flour or corn flour. Shake or stir.

Fill the puff pastry sheet with the fruit. Leave about 5 cm or 2 in on each side of the sheet and wrap the edges over the fruit (i.e. you pile the apple and pear topping in the middle, then fold over the edges).

Pop in the oven for about 15–25 minutes. You want to watch so that the edges of the puff pastry become brown and crispy, but don't burn.

Here's the deal—you can look up this recipe. There are lots of variations of it. But a tip when it comes to cooking is to find your own way of doing things. I love this recipe with plenty of lemon, but not so much sugar. Some people add butter to the fruit mixture. I like the spice a touch of ginger adds, some stick to just the cinnamon. Some brush their puff pastry edges with a whisked egg, but I don't think it's necessary. The important thing is to experiment and have fun!

What You've Learned in This Chapter

Whole foods are foods that haven't been processed much (i.e. something hasn't been removed or added) and are often considered the best foods to eat. Some call them natural foods.

By eating lots of whole foods, we get the building blocks (nutrients) we need for our body. That's why it's important to vary what we eat and eat lots of veggies, as well as smaller amounts of whole grains, nuts, beans and pulses, fruit, berries, dairy, eggs, meat, and fish.

Processed foods, like candy and crisps, are best in small amounts for celebrations and special occasions.

When you cook a meal, it's a good thing to first ask an adult what equipment you need and how to use it. Before you use a stove, microwave, or sharp knife, you always have to ask how to use it. It's also important to check what things you can use in an oven or microwave. Some things, like metal, can make a microwave break, while plastic will melt in an oven.

A good way of learning how to cook is asking your family for the "secret family recipes" and learning from the different people who love cooking them!

Another good way to get started in the kitchen is to create simple healthy treats. From there, you can move on to cooking proper meals.

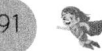

CHAPTER ELEVEN

Saving, Spending, and Other Money Matters

Learn to save and invest instead of spend and lose

What's the first thing to know about spending and saving? It all adds up!

---***---

Linda bought one hot chocolate from the school cafeteria every day. She didn't think much about it, because it only cost a dollar.

"That's such a waste of pocket money," Dan protested one day. "You could just ask your gran to make you one in the morning and bring it in a thermos."

"But then I have to carry the thermos around with me!"

"Sure, but now you buy five hot chocolates per week—one for every school day."

"So what? I like hot chocolate. And I don't buy a lot of other things in the cafeteria. I bring lunch."

"Five hot chocolates per week is five dollars per week. About twenty dollars per month. $240 per year. I know so many things I could buy for that money."

Linda became thoughtful.

"Also, if you put it in a bank account for a year and get 5% interest, it's an extra ten dollars or so on top. Not that much, but something."

---***---

Buying hot chocolate for two hundred odd dollars per year might not be so much. But imagine if there are a few things you spend five dollars per week on without thinking. Perhaps you

Saving, Spending, and Other Money Matters

spend $5 on candy, $5 on some subscription app, and $5 on a toy. Now it's $15 per week.

That's about $60 per month or $720 or so per year.

The point isn't that we shouldn't spend money.

It's about knowing *where* you spend it.

And what you really want. Perhaps you think spending the money on those things is worth it. Then keep spending them. But if you would prefer to save up and spend them on something else, then do that!

The Jar Method: Knowing Where Your Money Goes

"What are you doing with all those jars?"

"I'm deciding how to spend my money."

"But they are *jars*. How do they help you with how to best spend your money?"

"Well, I just got a job. Now, I have enough money to both spend *and* save. I want to buy so many things, but if I use all my money in one go, I won't have any money for later. So I decided to have three jars. One for the money I can spend now, one for things I want to save up to, like a camera, and one for saving for the future. You know, for stuff I'm going to buy when I'm older, like a car."

"Oh, that's cool."

"Yeah. And I will put what I save in the bank. Then I get interest."

"What's that?"

"It's what they pay you for keeping your funds with them. Sometimes you get three percent, sometimes five, or more. That means if I put $100 in the bank for a year, I get $3–5 by the end of the year."

"That's not a lot."

"No, but if I have $100,000 there, it's $3–5,000."

"Now, THAT is a lot."

"Exactly. So I need to save up $100,000."

Some really smart person way back when realized that you can divide the money you earn to keep better track of it. And stop yourself from spending it all in one go.

How do you do it?

You put the money in different jars.

You start by writing down all the things you NEED to buy for the month. Stuff like food, electricity, water, wifi, and so forth. That's your budget. And once you've worked out what that is, you write that number down.

That's the money you put in your spending jar.

Then you create one jar for fun stuff. Like going to the movies or paying for music streaming services and gaming apps. Here you can decide how much you're willing to spend every month on the fun stuff. Then you can see what you can actually afford to do for that amount.

That's your fun jar. Some people combine this with the spending jar. So it's just the one jar.

Then there are two more jars—one for short-term savings and one for long-term savings.

> Short-term savings can include anything from going to the dentist to buying a bike.
>
> Long-term savings can be things like saving up for college, buying a car, or your retirement funds.

You can get as creative as you like with it—have as many jars as you like. For example, one jar could be what you spend now. Like stuff you want to buy.

Another jar could be your short-term savings jar—things you'd like to buy that cost a bit more, like a new game console.

Then, you could divvy up the future spending jars. Have one for your college fund, one for future dream buys, like houses and cars, one for emergencies (like needing to get a new chain for your bike), and one for your retirement.

Yeah, really, your retirement. So you can quit your day job and do whatever you like when you want to.

Some people add an extra jar for charity. Like they might put a little bit of money aside every month and then for Christmas hand out gifts to the homeless. Or they set aside a budget every month for baking cookies for the homeless, or making treats for the dogs in the nearest rescue shelter.

You don't have to set aside money to give to others, that's your choice, but it can be a fun thing to do. Other people prefer to donate their time instead, and once a week, or once a month, volunteer with a local charity.

Why do we give our time to good causes?

Well, research has shown that it makes us happy, helps us bond with other people, and might even make us live longer!

Budgeting: Knowing How to Spend Well

I mentioned you need a jar for your spendings. But why bother to calculate what you spend your money on? Why not just pay for everything and save what's left?

Well, sometimes we buy things we can't afford. Only, we don't realize it until afterwards. And then we're in trouble.

Sometimes, big trouble.

We need budgets so that we know what we can afford.

It's actually very easy to buy things we *don't* need otherwise. Ever been to a grocery store when you were hungry and thrown stuff into your shopping basket randomly?

Most of us have. And as a kid, you can do that if your parents have given you money to spend on whatever you want, but as an adult, if you buy lots of treats at the beginning of the month (like throwing lots of candy, crisps, and ice cream into that basket), you might realize you don't have enough money for proper food at the end of the month.

Budgets are also good because they remind us of things we need to buy in the future.

Your bicycle is working now, but it won't work forever. If you don't save money for repairs, you won't have the money for it when you need it!

Everything we own wears out, so we need to set aside money to repair and replace it.

So the regular stuff we need, like food and electricity, aren't the only things we need to budget for!

Exercises to Try

Sit down with an adult and create a budget for buying a dog. What would it cost if you were to buy a dog, feed it, pay for vet insurance, buy it toys and other dog stuff?

You can also look at a monthly budget for living expenses if you'd like to find out all the stuff adults have to pay for (it's a lot).

On a piece of paper, draw some jars. Then decide what you want to fill them with money for. Do you just want three jars (spending money, short-term savings, and long-term savings), or do you want more jars for special stuff?

If you get pocket money or earn money by doing chores, you can get real jars and start using them. Some banks even let you create jars in your account!

What You've Learned in This Chapter

Money tends to be spent on all sorts of things if we don't keep an eye on it.

To keep track of our money, we make budgets. That way we know how much money we actually need for something. We also know what we need to set aside for emergencies and long-term goals.

One way to keep track of our money is to create jars.

The easiest jar system is three jars—one for spending, one for short-term savings, and one for long-term savings. You can have more jars to keep better track of your money.

CHAPTER TWELVE

Owning Your Time: Time Management and Study Skills

Master your time so you can have more free time

Time is like money—if you don't budget for it, it disappears.

Really? Time disappears?

Well, think about it. You sit down with your tablet, or phone, to look at an image. But then you see that game app you like. You start playing a game. Next time you look up, an hour has passed!

It's the same with social media. You logged onto your social media account to reply to a friend's message, but you started scrolling through your feed. You only meant to reply to that one message . . . but you spent an hour looking at updates and videos.

Oops.

That's why adults who get a lot done tend to have diaries or daily planners and plan their time. It can also help you do things *faster*.

Remember the chapter about chores?

When you have something boring to do, like making your bed (if you find that as boring as I do), you can set a timer on your phone or tablet, or use an egg timer. You can also buy different hourglasses that you use for different tasks or chores.

Scheduling Like a Pro—Making Time Work for You

Remember the chapter about goals?

> What are your goals this week? What are the things you need to do (like study for tests, homework, chores, etc.) and what are the things you want to do?
>
> That's the first thing to figure out.
>
> The second thing you need to know is when to do them.

This can also help break things down so tasks don't become so tedious. I prefer cleaning the house for 15 minutes per day, instead of cleaning for almost two hours one day every week.

If you find one subject in school really boring, breaking it down so you study for a few minutes at a time can help you get it done. You have to sit down for long enough to learn something, but you don't have to keep at it for an entire hour!

It's also important to think about what you want to get done during the time you have.

For example, if you know you have all day to complete a task, you take your time with it. As a result, it takes longer to get it done.

But if you have only fifteen minutes to do math and decide you want to do three equations during that time, you push yourself to get it done faster.

That way, you spend less time on the stuff you find boring, but still get it done!

The funny thing is, when you set goals like that and push yourself, sometimes boring tasks become fun!

Another reason for planning your time? You know what's coming next so you don't have to think about it.

If you've planned what homework you need to focus on for the week, you just look in your diary to see what's next on any given day.

If you haven't planned it? You start thinking about what subjects you have the next day, what the teachers said, and so forth. And while you're doing it, you might go check your phone and oops, there went twenty minutes as you started scrolling on your phone.

When we plan upfront, instead of figuring things out as we go, we save time. And the more time we save, the more time we have for that other stuff we want to do. Like hanging out with friends or riding our skateboard. Making videos. Taking photos. Whatever it is you enjoy doing!

Exercise

Sit down with an adult and schedule your week ahead. Put in the exact time you will spend on different homework assignments and chores every day, as well as any doctor's appointments or activities you need to attend for the week. For example, if you start studying at 4:00 p.m. every afternoon, write down what subject you will study first and for how long. Mark it in your diary or planner. Also add in what chores you will do and how long you will spend on them.

Don't forget to write down when you will do the things you love. Like painting a picture, making a video, or visiting a friend. Schedule in the time for that, too.

Sharpen Your Mind: Focus and Concentration

I'm currently reading a book called *Peak Mind* by Dr. Amishi P. Jha. Dr. Amishi is someone who studies how the brain works. In the book, she speaks about a mindfulness expert who has trained their mind for many, many years. Yet, the longest they said they could focus on only one thing? Seven seconds.

Seven seconds!

Our minds aren't great at focusing. And they get worse if we try to do many things at once (that's called multi-tasking) or look up every time our phone pings.

If you want to get something done fast, put away everything else.

Turn off the TV/laptop/radio/phone/tablet. Or walk into a room where you don't have access to them.

You especially want to put phones and tablets out of reach when you study. Otherwise, chances are you look up every time you get a notification. And if you do that, getting your homework done can take much, much longer.

Plus, if you frequently shift your focus, it's harder to learn. Your thoughts are constantly interrupted.

Just imagine. You're trying to read something. But every ten seconds, your brother or someone else screams. Every time that happens, you're distracted from the text. By the time you get to the bottom of the page, it's harder to get a grasp of what you just read.

So when you study, go somewhere quiet and open your books.

Feeling fidgety? Here are some tips to sharpen your focus. If you want to stay focused while studying, do this *before* you start.

- Prep a small snack that will provide energy for some time, like a slice of brown bread with hummus topped with tomatoes, peppers, or cucumber and perhaps a boiled egg, or piece of tofu
- Go for a ten- to twenty-minute run, very brisk walk, dance around the living room, or practice dribbling a ball (anything that gets your blood pumping, basically)
- Splash your face and, if you can handle it and DON'T HAVE A HEART CONDITION, the rest of your body in cold water (just make sure to wrap up warm afterwards)
- Eat the snack you prepped
- Sit down and take deep breaths in through your nose and out through your mouth, focusing your attention on your breathing. Your mind *will* wander but bring it back to your breathing. Do this for 3–5 minutes
- Start studying in a room with little to no distractions (definitely no phones or tablets) and have an alarm set for the different things you need to accomplish (for example, if you start with math, after fifteen minutes the alarm sounds to alert you to change and start studying English)

This takes up about thirty to sixty minutes of your time, depending on how long you exercise for and if you need to make your own snack. So it's the perfect routine after coming home from school and just before you start studying. If you walked home and it took twenty minutes, you've already done the exercise!

If you like studying while listening to music, choose something with no vocals. You don't want to be distracted by words. It seems jazz, classical music, or some sort of meditative music works best when we want to concentrate on a task.

If you have a lot of studying to do, make sure you stand up, shake it loose, and then sit down and take a few deep breaths every 30 minutes or so.

Want to improve your focus in general? Meditate. There are a ton of apps for this purpose with some offering music to relax to, which can be used when studying. Get an adult to help you download the right meditation app for you. You can also simply close your eyes and focus on your breath, as in the exercise above.

Tip: Challenge one of your parents, guardian, or any other adult to join you in this concentration exercise. Chances are, the adults in your life also have things they need to concentrate on that they've been putting off. Such as doing paperwork.

Another thing to remember if you want to keep your focus on top? Keep your body and brain in tip-top shape. For your body and brain to function, you need to:

- Go to bed and wake up around the same time every day
- Make sure you get enough hours of sleep (changes with age, about 9–12 hours till you're about 12, 8–10 hours in your teens, and 7–9 hours as an adult)
- Eat plenty of whole foods (natural foods) and LOTS of veggies

- Exercise for *at least* 20–40 minutes per day, or three hours per week if you divvy it up to three sessions
- Spend at least twenty minutes outdoors every day to get sunshine (and you actually catch rays even on cloudy days—you don't have to be *in* the sun; if you're actually in the sun, wear sunscreen to prevent skin cancer later in life)
- Spend at least two hours per week in nature (that's about 20 minutes per day if you go for daily walks, but you can also go to the beach, for a hike, or do something else that's fun to do in nature once a week)
- Meditate or do breathing exercises for 10–20 minutes per day
- Spend time having fun with friends and family (socialize . . . because believe it or not, it affects our health in a positive way!)

You and a friend or parent could challenge each other to make sure you do the above!

What are things you could do in nature that could be fun? Here are a few suggestions:

- Fly a kite
- Build a treehouse
- Go swimming
- Fly a drone
- Collect seashells
- Go fishing
- Bring an easel and make a painting
- Hike
- Play soccer (or any other sport)
- Bike
- Climb
- Slackline

Owning Your Time: Time Management and Study Skills

Boy: I heard you have to exercise for twenty minutes per day.

Girl: I heard you have to spend at least twenty minutes outside every day.

Boy: I heard you need to meditate for ten minutes every day.

Girl: I also heard you should spend time in nature, not just.

Boy: That's A LOT of time spent doing stuff for your health.

Girl: Maybe not.

Boy: It IS.

Girl: But what if you bike to school every day, through nature. And you bike for 20 minutes. Then you spend time outdoors, and you exercise. So it's only 20 minutes. And you can sit down and catch your breath for ten minutes when you get home. That's the meditation. And you're done!

Boy: You're clever.

Girl: Thanks.

What You've Learned in This Chapter

To get stuff done, you schedule it in your diary—writing down what time you'll do it and how much time you'll spend on it. You can set a time every Sunday to schedule the week ahead.

If you find something boring or simply difficult to focus on, break it down and spend shorter amounts of time on it in one go.

When you start your work, set a goal. Such as reading to a certain page, doing a certain amount of equations, or cleaning a certain number of rooms. This will help engage you in the task and push you to achieve it!

If you find it hard to focus, do some form of exercise for 10–20 minutes, splash your face (or your body) with cold water, have a healthy snack, take a few deep breaths, focusing your attention on your breathing, and then start your work.

Be sure to do tasks that require your focus in a room with little to no distractions, if possible. If you want to block out noise, you can use noise-blocking headphones or listen to some music. Choose music without vocals (or you'll get distracted by the words).

Exercising, eating well, spending time in nature, and sleeping well also help our brain and body stay happy. So does socializing and getting a little bit of sunshine every day. That, in turn, can help us become better at focusing.

Want to unleash your super focusing skills? Meditate. All it takes is a couple of minutes per day. It can be as easy as sitting down for ten minutes and focusing on your breathing!

CHAPTER THIRTEEN

Digital Superheroes: Navigating the Online World Safely

Learning how to deal with social media, AI, and a few other things in the online jungle

Your parents, or your grandparents, might still remember a time when all they had to connect with their friends was the phone.

The kind that hangs on a wall.

Or they would send a letter that took days, or weeks, to reach their friends or family.

Does that sound boring?

Well, perhaps, but it also meant that when you spoke to someone, you spoke *only* to them. And they couldn't easily share it.

Now, when you send a message to someone they can screenshot it and share it with the entire world with just one click. A lot easier than making photocopies of a letter and posting it all over town! And even then, it'd just be all over town—not all over the world.

Back in the day, when you took photos, you shared them just with friends and family. Now, everyone you know on Instagram, Facebook, and other social media platforms can see the photos you take. And, just as with messages, photos can be screenshot and shared.

This is something you need to remember: whatever you post online, even if you just post it to your friends, can be shared with people you don't know.

Social media is sort of like a public message board to the world.

Which is great for your public newsfeed—when you want to reach lots of people—but not so good when you're having private conversations and someone decides to share them.

I'm not saying your friends *will* share your photos and conversations, but they might. Plus, you don't know who is sitting beside them when they are using social media.

The bottom line? If you want to say something personal, save it for a phone call or in-person chat.

> "I sent a message to Ellie saying I don't like John. She screenshotted it and sent it to Mike, who sent it to John. And it was all a typo! I meant to write that I don't like JOHNNY."

Social Media Anxiety

When you post something to social media, it's usually the best stuff. Because no one wants to show the bad stuff.

That makes sense, because we show what makes us happy. The problem? A lot of people hide how they are really feeling. Then they feel bad because their real life isn't as cool as they've portrayed it to be online!

Others get anxious because they want to have as nice a life as someone else seems to have . . . at least on social media.

And let's face it: we aren't all stars when it comes to taking pictures and writing posts! Even if we lead an amazing life, it might not look great in our social media feed!

The thing is, you don't have to ace your social media feed.

You don't even need to have one! The most important thing is to create a life you actually enjoy.

How do you do that?

You write a list of all the things you enjoy doing. Then you open your diary and start scheduling the things you enjoy doing. Perhaps call some friends or relatives to engage them in activities, too!

Don't know what you enjoy? Ask friends, parents, and even teachers what activities they think you should try. Trying new activities can also help you meet new people. This is especially important if you don't have a lot of friends at school.

> Girl 1: She has a much better feed than me, I'm such a loser.
>
> Girl 2: My social media feed looks so much better than my life, I'm such a fake!
>
> Girl 3: I hate posting on social media, so I never do. Everyone must think I'm strange!

When to Post, When Not to Post

You might think the best time to post on social media is when you're over the moon about something. You just can't contain your happiness.

That's wonderful, but wait to post till you've had a moment.

Why?

Because when we're overexcited, we overreact. We might say things we later regret.

Sometimes we also have bad moments.

Back in the day, you called a friend and ranted about it. Or turned up the radio. Now . . . we post online. And then we regret it.

Here's a good rule: think before you post.

If you feel super excited or super down, chances are you'll exaggerate your post. Instead of posting when you feel like that, go for a run and *then* post. Better yet, go for a run, splash some cold water on your face, breathe for five minutes, and *then* post. By then, you should be feeling a lot more normal. You can also do other things, of course, such as watching a movie that changes your state of mind.

Besides, if you're upset about something, is the best place to discuss it online? Or is it something you should talk to friends and family about? Perhaps after doing that, you still want to post. But first, turn to the people who are close to you and talk it through.

> Boy posting on social media: "I got accepted to the Bears for the next hockey season. I'm like totally the best hockey player in my entire class and probably yours, too."
>
> Dad standing next to the boy: "Don't you think you're exaggerating a bit? If you post that, maybe you'll regret it when you see Ken tomorrow who also plays hockey and wasn't accepted to the Bears."

Connecting with Cool People and Controlling Your Privacy

If you're really into something, be that biking or acrobatics, you can find others online who publish content in that niche. You might even start making your own content. That could lead to making friends or even creating a career.

You can also have different accounts. One for something like fishing or dancing and another that's your personal account where you connect with friends you know in the real world.

On the account that's only for friends and family, you can share personal photos, and on the other account, you can share content related to your hobby.

This is also good if you live in a place where you feel you aren't part of the "it" crowd. By having an account people at school aren't aware of, you can make friends outside of school without taking your classmates' prejudice with you.

The other thing to remember is that even if you use just one account, you can control *who* you become friends with and *who* sees your posts. You have to go to your profile and change your privacy settings to ensure only friends see your content (if that's what you want). For example, you might want to share a photo of your latest dance show with anyone (a public post), but you only want the photos from a family dinner to be seen by friends.

That's important. You need to know who has access to your posts. So get an adult to help you check it out.

On some social media platforms, you can even create lists among your friends so you can choose who of your friends can see what posts you share. For example, you can make a list for all your gaming friends so that they are the only ones who see your posts about gaming. You can make another list of your school friends, so they are the only ones who see posts about school-related stuff. Or, perhaps, you wish to make sure they *don't* see your family photos.

Imagine looking at a funny (i.e. not cool) photo of you and your baby sister.

"Oh, darling, that's such a cute photo of you and your sister."

"Mom, I look insane."

"No, it's cute. Post it on Facebook so Auntie Elsie can see it."

"Sure, Mom."

Then you whisper, "I'll post it so Auntie Elsie and NO ONE ELSE can see it."

Negative Comments and Posts

If someone is downright rude to you online, what do you do?

Reacting in kind and being rude back usually solves very little. You sink to their level and might end up in a back-and-forth of rude or negative comments.

Instead, first screenshot the comment so you have proof it happened, should the person later remove it.

Secondly, consider if ignoring it isn't the best practice. Showing you don't care about their comment will show them they hold no power over you.

If you want to address something (and sometimes you have to as it's NOT all right if someone is being downright mean), you can try something along the lines of "Maybe you should think before you write comments like that. I don't need your approval to feel good about my posts, but dude, that's low. If you keep it up, I'll block you, but I hope I don't have to. We've known each other for a long time."

Sometimes, rather than responding to a comment, it's better to call someone to talk about it, or call their parents, or even a teacher, if necessary.

The best thing to do? Chat with some adult or older friend before responding. Someone who you know won't overreact but deal with it calmly. That way, you can ball some ideas and then decide on what to do. However, at the end of the day, you need to do what you know is right in your heart.

Whether or not you talk to someone else first, if you want to respond to a comment, take a moment before you do so. In fact, remember what I said about posting when you're happy or upset? Yep. Go for a run or a walk. Splash some cold water on your face. Have something to eat. Or simply go do something else for a while—watch a movie, hang out with friends, play with the dog. Then, take some deep breaths. Focus your mind. Then, when you know you're calm, respond.

If it keeps happening—if someone is continuously rude—you have to take action. The best practice is usually to block someone. If you don't know how, ask an adult.

If things have gone so far that you feel you're being harassed by a person, or a group of people, you have got to bring it up with an adult. You can even get protection orders if people continually bully you online, especially if they are threatening to harm you.

If someone's comments are sort of funny, sort of nasty, and you don't know how to deal with their comments, chat with an adult about it. They can help you decide how to deal with it.

This isn't just about others being rude to you—you have to remember not to be rude to others when you post online.

Talking down to someone online is as bad as in the real world. Don't do it.

The best rule? If you have nothing good to say, don't say it.

It's hard as a kid sometimes to see it this way (because often we are stuck with people at school), but if someone is nasty, they are the one with the problem. You don't want them in your life. And their opinion does not determine who you are or how you feel about yourself.

Act, not in reaction to others, but as who you want to be.

AI—Artificial Intelligence

Machines have started thinking for us. Sort of. AI is super exciting. Why? Because it can help us with so many things.

Just imagine popping all exciting medical data into a machine and having AI analyze it. You can see trends you've never seen. Find missing links. Make connections. Come up with new cures.

It's also exciting if you're studying.

Okay, *exciting* might not be the right word for how everyone feels, but it's certainly *useful*. For example, let's say you want to write an essay about the origins of Santa Claus. Yep, he didn't just arrive on a sled drawn by reindeer one fine day. There are myths and legends that sort of collided to create what we today know as Santa. And thank goodness for that or we'd all have boring Christmases, Yuletides, or whatever it is you celebrate around that time of year when you get gifts.

Anyway, you want to write a great essay, so you go to ChatGPT and ask it questions about Santa. Like where the legend originated. You ask it to be described in such a way a ten-year-old can understand it easily (if you're ten).

And there you have it. It answers in a way that's easy to understand. And if you don't understand the answer or some part of the answer, you just tell ChatGPT to rewrite it, or ask questions about what you don't understand.

You didn't have to check ten books to get the information. AI just provided it to you on a platter.

That said . . . a lawyer not long ago used ChatGPT to come up with arguments for court and got it all wrong.

> You have to double-check your facts.
>
> Once you get the facts from ChatGPT, cross-refer with Gemini (the AI app developed by Google), and then google them, or look up the information at a local library. See if it seems like the facts you have add up.

Fact checking doesn't take as long as reading a ton of material to get the answer in the first place. That's why AI is making life easier.

As a writer, I use AI a lot. Sometimes I ask ChatGPT or Gemini to correct a sentence I've written. Sometimes I ask for information. Let's say I'm writing a novel about a dairy farmer, but I know nothing about cows. Now, all I have to do is ask AI what the day-to-day life of a dairy farmer looks like instead of reading a ton of blogs or books to try to work it out. Likewise, I can ask an AI app what someone would say over the intercom when landing a plane in Alaska during a snowstorm (yes, I once asked ChatGPT that and it helped me come up with the dialogue!).

AI is a tool for helping you with work and schoolwork, but it's not the only tool. You have to use your own brain and other resources, too.

Of course, you *could* ask ChatGPT to write an entire essay for you.

But should you?

No.

You can ask ChatGPT what it thinks you should include in the essay and why.

You can ask ChatGPT to help you structure the essay and ask why it suggests the structure it does.

That's great. You're learning while you're using it.

If, on the other hand, you ask ChatGPT to write the essay for you, you don't learn, and of course there's also a chance that ChatGPT gets some of the information wrong.

But it's just an essay, right? And you plan to become a mechanic, so why would you need to learn to write essays?

Well, because it helps you structure information.

You might not want to write an essay about Santa, but doing so teaches you to do research, check facts, and argue a point, or simply come to a conclusion.

When your customer asks you to fix their car and replace car parts, you have to research the best way to repair the car, the best and cheapest car parts, and argue why they should choose you as their mechanic over the competition.

School tasks often help us understand how to think about things. It's not just about doing the task at hand, it's about the stuff you learn while doing it.

Perhaps the above example about the mechanic isn't that relatable to everyone, but in life, there are countless times when you have to gather facts, come up with a conclusion, and present it to others.

And to prevent works being created by ChatGPT and other AI tools, there are "AI checks" these days. Your teachers can check your essay and find out if it was written by AI, or not.

AI can help a lot with science and development, and it's fabulous for research. You can use it to edit grammar for your school assignments. And people use it to learn languages. Some AI solutions can even help create or edit photos for projects or for social media.

AI is also great for coming up with ideas. Ask ChatGPT or Gemini for some ideas for science projects, businesses to start, or plots for a book—then take the best ideas and develop them by doing further research.

There are so many things AI can help you with. If you get stuck on a sentence, you can ask an AI app to write it for you. If you don't understand a passage in your biology book, you can ask an AI app to describe it to you using different wording. I only wish I'd had AI when I was struggling with chemistry back in high school! My teacher was a dead bore (I'm sorry, but truly, he was) and it would have helped make chemistry fun!

AI is great. You just have to make sure you don't use ONLY AI when working on stuff.

And here's the other thing: anything you feed to AI stays with AI unless it states somewhere in the privacy policy of the app that you're using that it doesn't.

If you tell an AI app your life story, it will be uploaded to its "brain" (information cloud might be a better description) and stay there. So that when other people ask questions, your story could end up in their answers.

What You've Learned in This Chapter

What you share in a message or a post on social media can be screenshotted and shared with others.

Put yourself in a calm state of mind before you post anything or send messages online. If you're overexcited or upset, chances are you'll regret what you're about to say as it's going to be exaggerated. You can even have a rule to always wait at least five to fifteen minutes before you respond to anything, but if you're upset, you have to take a proper break and go do something else before posting or responding.

If you feel bad about something, consider chatting to someone about it instead of writing a post on social media.

If someone says negative stuff to you on social media, screenshot it for proof, then ignore it if it isn't a big deal. If you wish to respond, chat with a calm adult about it, or at least take some time to calm down yourself before responding.

Don't sink to the level of the people saying negative things. Be someone whom you're proud of when responding.

If someone says something truly nasty that needs addressing, always speak to an adult about it. You can't ignore certain content—it needs to be dealt with.

If someone continues to post negative things about you, block them and talk with an adult about it.

On social media, you decide who sees your posts—everyone, friends, or only certain friends. Go through your privacy settings with an adult to learn how to control who sees what.

You can create more than one account on places like Instagram and TikTok, so if you have a special interest, such as soccer or dancing, you can create a special account for your hobby. That way you can meet like-minded people.

Know that what people post on social media isn't the full truth. People usually take a picture of the side of their bedroom that's been cleaned and looks nice—not the corner where they keep their dirty laundry.

AI is brilliant for research, checking your grammar, getting ideas, having difficult passages in textbooks explained to you, and some other stuff. But using only AI means you don't truly learn as you aren't doing your job—you're letting AI do it for you. It also means your teachers are likely to find out as there are tools for that.

With AI, it's important to remember that what you say to the machine stays in the machine. Protect your privacy!

CHAPTER FOURTEEN

Becoming an Eco-Warrior: Protecting Our Planet Together

Learn how to treat the Earth like your home, not a waste garden

Earth is your home.

This is where you live.

It should be treated like a palace. Just like your body, which is housing you. Without either, you'd be lost.

Nature needs us to pay attention. Because if not, we pay the price. If we pollute the rivers and eat the fish in them, we end up polluted. And as it stands, there's a lot of pollution.

Not only that, it seems like we produce so much carbon dioxide and methane that the temperature of the planet is going up! Some say this is because we're heading for the next ice age (and not because of pollution) but carbon dioxide and methane aren't great for you, that's for sure. Plus, if the temperature goes up too much, it causes havoc with the weather, kills off animals, and might sink cities as the ice on the South Pole and North Pole is melting.

Our whole ecosystem might come apart. And that means plants, animals, and even humans can die. In fact, some humans and animals have already died from toxins leaking out into rivers and other places.

Mother: "Oh, look there's a honeybee. That's great."

Boy: "Why is it great? They sting. And some people are allergic and get really sick."

Mother: "Bees are good because they pollinate flowers. That's needed for plants to produce seeds and fruits which in turn produce more plants. Without bees and bumblebees, there'd be little to no flowers, fruits, vegetables, and so on. The plants produce oxygen that we need to breathe. And we eat a lot of the plants. So without the bees, humans might no longer survive. That's why it's called an ecosystem—if one plant or animal dies out, it affects all the others."

Boy: "Let's plant some flowers in our garden for the bees."

Apart from looking after the bees, what can you do to save the planet?

It's not as hard as you'd think, because every little bit helps.

Practical Steps for Environmental Superheroes

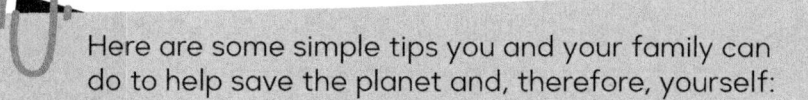

Here are some simple tips you and your family can do to help save the planet and, therefore, yourself:

1. Switch to LED lights (or talk to your parents about doing it)
2. Turn off any lights you don't need or once you're done using them
3. Use a good electricity provider, one that uses as much green energy as possible . . . ask your parents about what you're using at home!
4. Don't buy more than you need
5. Buy secondhand clothing or clothing that lasts a long time. You can also find clothing made in eco-friendly ways (usually shops have "conscious collections")
6. Buy things like furniture and toys secondhand

7. Buy stuff made from recyclable or eco-friendly materials
8. Use environmentally friendly body products and cleaning products (that also saves you from being exposed to chemicals!). Learn to read labels, like we talked about for food. If you aren't sure what they are, ask an adult to go shopping with you to find them
9. Buy pesticide-free/wild/organic food—if you can't afford buying everything that way, buy some that way
10. Eat things that are in season so that greenhouses aren't needed to grow them, or they don't need to be shipped around the globe to get to you
11. Buy local products (so that they aren't shipped around the planet before you get them)
12. Avoid buying palm fruit oil unless it's rainforest-friendly (it might say that it's sustainable and then it's okay)
13. Use a compost—throw all food waste in there and turn it into soil
14. Harvest rainwater to use at home and/or use as little water as possible (take quick showers instead of baths—even challenge yourself to use a bucket to clean yourself)
15. Read magazines and books online or buy secondhand books. You can also check the library!
16. Recycle your waste—glass, plastic, paper, and metals, as well as batteries can be recycled
17. If you use paints, glues, and other crafts materials, buy eco-friendly ones
18. Use public transport or a bike instead of your own car, but if your family has a car, carpool (or encourage your parents to do so—you can even challenge them to walk or bike with you to school!)
19. Try and avoid packaging—many stores these days encourage you to buy stuff to put in your own containers!
20. Look into more ways to offset your carbon footprint (or ask ChatGPT about it!)

Exercise

Write down five things you can do to become an eco-warrior! And put it in your diary or planner as goals so that you remember to actually do them!

Girl: "Why do you have buckets in the shower, Mom?"

Mom: "I use them to wash myself."

Girl: "Silly, there's a shower."

Mom: "When I turn on the shower it's nice. I stay in here for a long time. But here I have five buckets. I use two to get wet. Three to clean myself after applying shampoo and conditioner. That saves A LOT of water."

What You've Learned in This Chapter

If you pollute nature, you often end up polluting yourself—you breathe the polluted air or eat the polluted food.

Earth is an ecosystem, so if you damage one type of plant or animal, it has a knock-on effect on the rest of the life forms on Earth.

Buying secondhand, buying local foods that are in season, and buying eco-friendly cleaning and body products can help you become an eco-warrior. So can recycling and composting, using as little energy as possible (switching to LED lights, turning off lights you aren't using, using less water, and walking, biking, or using public transport instead of asking your parents or older siblings to drive you in their car).

You can't always live completely eco-friendly, just do what you can.

Let's say you can only afford to buy one LED light right now, not exchange all the lights in your home. Well, if everyone did that, billions of lightbulbs would be exchanged.

Every little bit helps!

Conclusion

Your Super Skills Journey Continues

There is soooooo much to learn in life.

This book contains a few of the things I hope will make your life easier, fulfilling, and more fun.

I hope it will make you happier and more confident by choosing the right stories to tell yourself about who you are and the stuff that happens to you.

I hope it will make you practice people skills so that you can more easily feel good about making new friends.

I hope it will make you think before you post on social media.

I hope it will help you choose the food you eat to ensure you get all those building blocks that will help your body grow strong and healthy.

I hope it will make you healthier and happier by spending time outdoors, exercising, and meditating.

I hope it will make you experiment with how to get your chores and studies done as fast and efficiently as possible.

I hope it will make you play around in the kitchen so you slowly learn to become a great chef.

And I hope it will make you curious about things like AI and eco-friendliness so you go out there and explore more while also being careful. Not all the information out there is true.

I also hope this book will make you talk to your parents or other adults you trust about the things you learn. So you can learn more or hear their opinions.

To get the most out of this book, you have to try the exercises. And it's best to tackle one chapter at a time, or it will feel like a lot of work. So go back and reread a chapter and do the exercise. The more you practice, the easier it'll get!

Printed in Great Britain
by Amazon